Contents

INTRODUCTION   1

CHAPTER 1 Sex and gender differences: a growth industry   4

    Part 1: Setting the scene   4

             Grounds for optimism   4
             Clarification of terms   5
             A bit of educational history   5

    Part 2: Sex differences and sexism   7

             Research surveys   7
             Sexism in schools   10
             The United States   12
             Feminist perspectives   13
             International studies   14
             The curriculum — overt and covert   14
             The Equal Opportunities Commission   16
             An afterthought   17

CHAPTER 2 The boy-girl imbalance in languages   18

         Public opinions   18
         Adult education   19
         The teaching profession   20
         New entrants to the teaching profession   22
         Research and higher degree courses   24
         First degree courses   25
         Examinations at 18+   27
         Examinations at 16+   30
         Choices at the option stage   35
         The first three years of FL learning   38

CHAPTER 3 Sex differences in language learning: myths and
           reality   41

    Focus 1: Biological and cognitive differences   41
    Focus 2: Affective factors   44

CHAPTER 4 Gender differences in school and the drop-out problem:
           causes and remedies   51

Factor 1: Status and provision   52

       Matriculation   52
       Examinations post-16   53
       Options   53
       Counselling   53
       Publicity   54
       French and other languages   54
       Setting by sex   57
       Proposed remedies   57

Factor 2: Teachers and teaching   59

       Staffing   59
       Teaching approaches   a) Didactics   61
                         b) The products of language
                           learning   62
                         c) The teacher's role   63
       Teaching materials and subject matter   64
       Assessment   66
       Proposed remedies   69

Factor 3: The pupils themselves   71

       Pupil-focussed remedies   78

CONCLUSION   80

BIBLIOGRAPHY   81

ACKNOWLEDGEMENTS

I should like to express my gratitude to several people who helped
in various ways in the production of this publication: to Gill Lewis
for her careful work on the typescript; to Julia Batters for her
assistance in the research field-work; to the pupils and teachers in
the schools who allowed us into their classrooms; to Sarah Death and
her colleagues at CILT who found facts and figures and gave good
advice; most of all to my wife, Margaret, for her constant
encouragement and common sense.

B.P.

Boys, girls and languages in school

Bob Powell

CILT

Centre for Information on Language Teaching and Research

CILT 28325 (subj) 486

(£3.95)

First published 1986
ISBN 0 948003 70 7
Copyright © 1986 Centre for Information on Language Teaching and
Research

Printed in Great Britain by Multiplex Techniques Ltd

Published by Centre for Information on Language Teaching and
Research, Regent's College, Inner Circle, Regent's Park, London
NW1 4NS

Introduction

The title of this Information Guide places boys before girls. There is a good alphabetical precedent for this sequence. However, some would argue that for far too long, in terms of educational needs and priorities, boys have tended to be considered first and girls second. Only relatively recently has the under-achievement of girls, notably in the sciences, become the focus of attention and research. Agencies such as the Equal Opportunities Commission have made it their duty to persuade more girls that it is an unwise step to drop science subjects. The campaign to encourage girls into careers in science and technology may not have been complemented by similar efforts to argue the case for boys studying languages, but it is a natural outcome of changing values and expectations in society. Heightened awareness of the restrictive nature of sex-stereotyping in school and work has led to genuine concern over pupils' choices of subjects in the curriculum.

But there is a real risk, in my view, that, with the increasing emphasis on science and technology for both boys and girls, the arts - and especially the language arts - will be neglected. For economic, social and cultural reasons it is important that pupils of both sexes see the value of a sustained course of foreign language study. Unfortunately, there is evidence to suggest that more and more pupils are abandoning language learning at the earliest opportunity. Some would blame this state of affairs on the nation which allows its politicians and business people to go around the world assuming that everyone must speak English, or the media which provide a voice-over translation every time foreigners dare to speak their own language. Others would point to the limited scope of the 'A' level system and unrealistic expectations of modern language examination syllabuses generally. Questions are also raised about the quality of teaching in our schools.

Whatever the reasons - and this Guide will attempt to unravel some of the possible causes - the drift away from languages is most marked among the boys. The decline is quite dramatic at Advanced level, but lower down the secondary schools, too, there are signs that the appeal of new scientifically related subjects and vocational courses is attracting many pupils away from languages.

So, it could be argued, it is timely to investigate why there is an imbalance between the sexes as far as foreign languages uptake is concerned and why, in particular, boys seem less likely to number among those pupils who gain advanced qualifications.

1

This brief Guide, therefore, sets out to do several things. Firstly, an attempt is made, through an analysis of relevant literature and policy decisions, to chart the growing concern for equality of educational opportunity for both sexes. Studies of sex differences in foreign language learning are scant, to say the least, compared with those in other areas of the curriculum and I shall report on personal investigations in this field.

Secondly, I shall examine the extent of the imbalance as manifested through all sectors of the educational pyramid, that is, from the foundations of secondary education through to the teaching profession itself.

Thirdly, mindful of the hazards laid for anyone entering the minefield of research into psychological sex differences and sex-role formation, I shall guide the reader to an examination of some of the claims and counter-claims produced by academics over the past ten years or so.

Fourthly, abandoning theoretical perspectives, I shall review current practice in our secondary schools. What are the factors that hinder and help equality of opportunity in foreign language education? Formal elements such as curriculum organisation will come under scrutiny, as will fluctuating variables such as prevailing pupil and teacher attitudes.

Finally, conscious of the need to inspire more pupils of both sexes to 'opt in', I shall propose certain practical remedies which, if implemented, might bring about an increase in the numbers of boys and girls studying a foreign language for longer than the present compulsory two or three years.

Ultimately, the person most likely to influence events is the practising teacher for whom the maxim must be:

> 'Equal opportunity for the boys and girls is an essential feature of good education practice.' (1)

I personally believe all pupils to be capable of deriving enjoyment and benefit from learning a foreign language. It is now time for a concerted effort to be made by policy-makers, curriculum planners, advisers, trainers and classroom practitioners. Foreign language education needs also to attract greater support from parents and careers counsellors. Language teachers need to make sure that their voices are heard in any debate about equality of opportunity. Otherwise, the drift away from languages, especially among the male student population, will continue inexorably to undermine all good intentions. To say that this would be a lamentable situation is an understatement. It would run counter to what most people perceive as a 'good education' - namely, the provision of opportunities for every pupil to develop his or her talents and skills to the full.

1. PRATT J, et al: <u>Option choice - a question of equal opportunity.</u>
    Windsor: NFER-Nelson (1984). Full bibliographical details of all
    subsequent references will be found in the bibliography at the
    end of the book.

1

Sex and gender differences: a growth industry

PART ONE: SETTING THE SCENE

Grounds for optimism

'We must assume that a substantial part of any human characteristic, be it "masculinity" or "intelligence" is cultural and
hence open to change' (Delamont, 1980, p7).

The above statement could have been presented as a neat conclusion
to this brief review of some of the literature on sex and gender
differences in education. Instead, I have decided to present it as
an optimistic preface - optimistic because, if we accept the all-
pervasive influence of social attitudes on children's concepts of
gender and gender roles and we believe that traditional divisions
between the sexes in areas of responsiblity and action are now
inappropriate, then we can set about changing attitudes and practice
within schools. This is, indeed, what some local authorities through
their initiation of equal opportunities projects have been seeking
to do. Many teachers in schools are also actively engaged in reviewing their curriculum policies and classroom procedures. Pupils themselves are challenging outdated assumptions about boys' and girls'
apparently differing needs.

All of this has not occurred by accident. It is largely the result
of vigorous campaigning especially by the Women's Movement. Our
awareness of the damaging effects of sex-stereotyping in education
has increased rapidly over the past few years. Attention has rightly
been directed mostly to the situation of girls, the principal aim
being, in curriculum terms, to increase the number of girls taking
sciences. It is only relatively recently that there has been any
serious consideration of the lost opportunities for boys in the
arts.

This Guide will attempt to strike an even balance between the sexes
in the distribution of words upon the page but I am conscious, as
every teacher must be, that as a direct consequence of the drift
away by boys from French, the main modern language taught in British
schools, the whole of foreign language education increasingly runs
the risk of being artificially labelled as 'feminine'. Besides,
dwindling numbers in the second foreign language class, made worse
by falling school rolls, present a real threat to second foreign
language provision overall. No language teacher can afford to be

complacent in the present climate. Yet, if we recognise that society's values are changing and that the changes can be hastened by concerted action among teachers and educationalists, then, I believe, there are grounds for optimism.

Clarification of terms

Sara Delamont provided me with a useful quotation to set this chapter in motion. She also provides the reader with a necessary clear definition of the distinction between the terms 'sex' and 'gender'.

> 'Sex should properly refer to the biological aspects of male and female existence. "Sex differences" should therefore only be used to refer to physiology, anatomy, genetics, hormones and so forth. Gender should properly be used to refer to all the non-biological aspects of differences between male and female - clothes, interests, attitudes, behaviours and aptitudes, for example, which separate "masculine" from "feminine" life styles' (Delamont, 1980, p5).

Not every writer on this subject during the last twenty years or so has adhered rigidly to this definition. The books that make up my selection of recommended reading present sometimes confused, sometimes confusing terminology. This Guide is probably no exception and I am probably as guilty as anyone in tending to use language in a neglectful way or glossing over details which may appear trivial yet may be crucial to a fuller understanding of this complex subject.

Whereas in the sixties and seventies it was customary to see researchers tackling the vexed question of sex differences in physical and cognitive development from a more clinical point of view, the tendency latterly has been to abandon pseudo-scientific empiricism in favour of observation, description and analysis of learning and learned behaviours in which there appear to be noticeable gender differences.

A bit of educational history

The vast majority of British children now experience secondary education in mixed comprehensive schools. This fact of life today is quite remarkable if we pause to consider the strength of opposition to co-education which characterised so much of the educational literature in the twenties, thirties and forties. Those opposed to mixed schooling in fact received renewed encouragement recently with the publication of the strongly argued Co-education reconsidered, edited by Rosemary Deem (Deem, 1984). There is also the fact that the comprehensive school as an institution has been - and continues to be - something of a political football. Yet it was only with the advent of comprehensive schools in large numbers during the sixties and seventies and the increase in the number of mixed schools subsequent to reorganisation that society began to question, albeit in a limited way, the differing values placed upon boys' and girls' education.

Successive official education reports and documents which paved the way for the 1944 Education Act did nothing to suggest that forty years later the single-sex state school would be the exception rather than the rule. Single-sex education seemed the only possibility for the nation's children who, it was assumed, would have vastly different career orientations and work experience. It seemed only natural that boys should emerge from schools, equipped to manage the economy, govern the nation, design the tools of industry, etc. Girls, on the other hand, were destined for less challenging roles. For example, in the Hadow Report of 1926 it was argued that they should be well versed in the intricacies of housewifery if Britain was to prosper! Later, in 1943, the Norwood Report was published. This was manifestly a document about the education of male pupils since the female of the species hardly deserved a mention as a group. This committee justified the inclusion of domestic subjects in the curriculum because, first and foremost, 'knowledge of such subjects is a necessary equipment for all girls as potential makers of homes' (Norwood Report, 1943).

The tripartite system proposed in the 1944 legislation was based, with a few exceptions, on the retention of single-sex schools with several obvious differences in curricular philosophy and provision being sustained. In 1963, the influential report of the Central Advisory Council for Education, better known as the Newsom Report, was published. This dealt specifically with pupils of average or less than average ability. In Part One in a section dealing with objectives we can read:

> 'This is a century which has seen and is still seeing marked changes in the status and economic role of women. Girls themselves need to be made aware of the new opportunities which may be open to them and both boys and girls will be faced with evolving a new concept of partnership in their personal relations, at work and in marriage' (Newsom Report, 1963, p28).

But this paragraph is rather a token acknowledgement of changing circumstances. The report elsewhere constantly links engineering, crafts and technical work with boys' aspirations (and hence curricular needs) while jobs in offices, in shops and in catering are the girls' destiny - not to mention what is dubbed 'their most important vocational concern, marriage'.

We have to wait until 1975 for a real challenge to the social and educational order. In the autumn of 1973 Her Majesty's Inspectors were requested by the government to undertake a study of 'the extent to which curricular differences and customs contributed to inequality of opportunity for boys and girls' (HMI, 1975).

The survey of secondary schools in England that resulted encompassed a 10% sample of maintained schools, statistically representative of the different sizes and types of secondary schools across the country and including, of course, single-sex and mixed arrangements. The ensuing publication Education Survey No. 21 provided hard evidence of the polarisation effects of curricular options especially, in numerical terms, with regard to the 'masculinity' of the sciences and the 'femininity' of language studies.

At last it began to dawn on people that the opportunities for early specialisation that the option stage provides in many British schools can be counter-productive. The HMI survey certainly sounded warning bells for all those who wished to hear. The report concluded in the following way:

> 'It may be that society can justify the striking differences that exist between the subjects studied by boys and girls in secondary schools, but it is more likely that a society that needs to develop to the full the talents and skills of all its people will find the discrepancies disturbing' (p24).

If it is believed that a broad, balanced curriculum including sciences and languages is desirable for all pupils, then stronger advice is needed to LEAs and schools. I suspect that the situation is little different ten years after publication of that report. If anything in the case of languages the polarisation effect is even more acute since the attraction of the sciences for both sexes has certainly increased.

PART TWO: SEX DIFFERENCES AND SEXISM

Research surveys

The developments in educational thinking mapped out briefly above have run parallel to, some would say have been strongly influenced by, research in the social sciences and psychology into perceived or supposed sex differences. Much of the early work in this field was conducted in the United States.

Recognised as something of an epic, The development of sex differences, edited by Eleanor Maccoby, was published in Britain in 1967. Here the key question of the relative influence of biological attributes and socialisation through culture was studied in depth by a survey of available research. The editor's own chapter on 'Sex differences in intellectual functioning' provides the following cautious conclusion:

> 'We find then that environmental effects are not merely something added to, or superimposed upon, whatever innate temperamental differences there are that affect intellectual function-

ing. Rather, there is a complex interaction. The two sexes would appear to have somewhat different intellectual strengths and weaknesses, and hence different influences serve to counteract the weaknesses and augment the strengths' (Maccoby, 1967, p51).

Later, collaborating with Carol Jacklin, Eleanor Maccoby produced the weighty volume The psychology of sex differences (Maccoby and Jacklin, 1974). This book was intended as a sequel to the earlier work and gathered together a massive array of evidence concerning how the sexes differ, or do not in fact differ, in many aspects of psychological behaviour. Their ambitious undertaking was to sift the relevant academic literature by now proliferating at a remarkable rate. They set themselves the task of determining which of the many conclusions made by researchers could be said to have a firm factual basis and which could be rejected as unproven or still equivocal. The annotated bibliography of research monographs which runs to 231 pages provides some fascinating insights about studies ranging from esoteric topics such as 'Sex differences in field dependence for the Eskimo' (there are none), to others probably more relevant as far as we are concerned, such as the effects of peer group behaviour on the different sexes (where boys were found to be more susceptible to friends' influence and persuasion than girls).

In their section dealing with intellectual abilities and cognitive styles they evaluated what they define as 'one of the more solidly established generalisations', namely the conventional view that females are superior to males in verbal tasks. They reviewed no fewer than 136 research studies spanning virtually the whole life cycle (3 months to 84 years). These covered aspects of language such as vocabulary naming and recognition, verbal imitation, fluency and reading comprehension. All experiments related to linguistic activities in the mother tongue although one or two involved bilingual children. There were no studies of foreign language acquisition.

It would be true to say that the work of Maccoby and Jacklin served to reinforce in the minds of educational academics and practitioners the traditional theory that differences really do exist, that they are minimal at primary school age, but that at around the age of ten or eleven girls come into their own in verbal performance. Conversely, it was reported that, in visual spatial tasks, boys have an advantage, their superiority tending to emerge in early adolescence – in some aptitude tests even earlier – and continuing into adulthood.

Almost as soon as their monumental work was published, Maccoby and Jacklin came in for a good deal of criticism. That was perhaps the inevitable consequence of their desire to summarise such a vast amount of evidence and draw their own conclusions at a time when the debate was intensifying with every new article published. Jeanne Block, in an erudite, persuasive and critical appraisal of their

work two years after it was published considered it to be 'a controversial portrayal of the field' (Block, 1976, p283). She also issued
timely advice to amateur researchers. There is always the risk that
the ill-informed may be too easily persuaded of the existence of
hard evidence to support already wellformed preconceptions - myths,
in other words. When someone has gone to the trouble of collecting
together sets of data for us and providing a neat structure on which
everything seems to fit, in our eagerness for conclusions we regard
the overall picture as more authoritative than is warranted. This is
particularly liable to occur if the topic under study is by its very
nature polemical, as investigations into sex differences are. In
Block's words:

> 'Lay people and even other scientists unfamiliar with the data
> being considered will not recognise sufficiently the provisional
> and debatable character of a particular organisation and inter-
> pretation of the available empiricism' (p286).

We have been warned!

Whatever our point of view, The psychology of sex differences made
an important contribution to better understanding of the complex-
ities of human nature. It did more than provide a digest of research
to date, it included a sensitive study of the major psychological
theories that purport to explain why sex differences should occur at
all. These they reduce to three comprehensible developmental theories. It is worth quoting here the abbreviated versions they include
in their introduction:

ORIGINS OF PSYCHOLOGICAL SEX DIFFERENCES

1) Through imitation: children choose same sex models (particularly
   the same sex parent) and use these models more than the opposite
   sex models for patterning their own behaviour. This selective
   modelling need not be deliberate on the child's part of course.

2) Through praise or discouragement: parents (and others) reward
   and praise boys for what they conceive to be 'boylike' behaviour
   and actively discourage boys when they engage in activities that
   seem feminine, similarly girls receive positive reinforcement
   for 'feminine' behaviour, negative reinforcement for 'masculine'
   behaviour.

3) Through self-socialisation: the child develops a concept of what
   it is to be male and female, and then, once he (or she) has a
   clear understanding of his (or her) sex identity, he (or she)
   attempts to fit his (or her) own behaviour to his (or her) concept of what behaviour is sex-appropriate.

Inevitably these theories have great relevance when we come to con-

9

sider questions specifically relating to foreign language education in Chapters 3 and 4; for example the extent to which same sex peer group pressure can be applied on potentially very able boy linguists causing them to abandon languages too early. Peer group evaluation of what is sex-appropriate can, of course, be very misleading. Then there is the extent to which the preponderance of women language teachers in some departments may influence pupils' image of foreign languages in school. There are also aspects of classroom interaction, pupil activity and behaviour in language lessons which have to be studied. The role of parents in the formation of children's attitudes to school subjects in general and languages in particular should not be overlooked. In fact, questions requiring answers spring to mind very easily.

But, to return for the moment to more general issues: the growth in sex difference research after Maccoby and Jacklin.

Most of the sex difference findings that they had reported were, in fact, incidental to the investigators' real research goals. They were, of course, fully aware of this and consequently urged that more and better research be carried out based on hypotheses that were explicitly intended to test sex differences. This exhortation, together with increasing dissatisfaction with the broad sweep of their conclusions, served to stimulate a flurry of research activity on both sides of the Atlantic.

When that research was directed more precisely at education – especially in studies involving the causal link between provision and outcomes – it added new impetus to the discussions that were being generated in the late seventies and early eighties about sexism in schools.

Sexism in schools

It is important to look at the theoretical basis and the concrete results of sexism and sex-role stereotyping, since the effects of these on a child's education far outweigh any consequence of biological or cognitive variations between the sexes assumed to exist or 'proved' to exist thus far. This is a personal view but I share this opinion with a growing number of commentators and researchers in the field.

With a few notable exceptions most major contributions to the literature on sexism have emanated and continue to emanate from women writers. This is hardly surprising since women have most to gain from exposing sexist practices. Some might add 'and men have most to lose', but that would be in itself a pitifully jaundiced view of changing social attitudes over the past twenty years. In the case of modern languages it is manifestly not true that boys would have most to lose. By conforming to stereotyped expectations, many boys have missed out on foreign language learning in school only to feel inadequate and frustrated later in life in their social and commercial contacts with people in other countries.

The brief review of texts that follows is bound to be selective and some may not agree with my choices. Those wishing to gain a more detailed analysis and broaden their selection of reading matter are advised to consult the bibliographies that are appended to these and other works. That is a daunting prospect since, in some cases, the list of titles consulted occupies as much as a quarter of the text.

I have restricted my comments on textual matters to complete volumes since these are probably the most accessible to readers. Hardly a week goes by now without some new research findings relevant to the study of gender differences or sexism being published in articles in the academic or professional journals. The variable of sex is now firmly embedded in most psychological, sociological or educational research design. However, rather than concentrate on the biological or evolutionary foundations for theories about sex differences in cognition and behaviour, writers in the early seventies began to press home the arguments about social and cultural conditioning. To the 'nature-nurture' debate that had been preoccupying the minds of social and clinical psychologists for many years was added this new element. The emphasis on explaining sex differences in terms of innate biological features such as sex hormones, or developmental characteristics such as cerebral assymetry brought with it the danger that, however unwarranted some of the claims, certain 'proofs' might be used to defend traditional sex roles. Given that Western societies were undergoing rapid changes in social customs and law affecting the sexes, it became essential to illustrate and explain how the 'natural order' for centuries past was ill-conceived, artificial and in its exclusion of women from positions of authority and decision-making, totally unacceptable. It was crucial for women commentators (and still is) to demonstrate the extent to which the institutions of our society had been designed and continued to function in a way likely to maintain, either by legislation or convention, traditional expectations about the status and roles of the two sexes.

As early as 1972 Corinne Hutt's <u>Males and females</u> made, at least according to the cover blurb, 'an important contribution to the debate on men, women and their fulfilment in society' (Hutt, 1972). Having spent time on the biological aspects, the author did produce a readable account of the social behaviours, interests, attitudes and predispositions that characterise the two sexes. Her focus tended to be the interests and activities of pre-school children, but she underplayed the effects of social conditioning in producing differences between the sexes. During her discussion of aggression, affiliation and ambition she reviewed research in a number of countries and she concluded that since similar behaviours were observable in a number of different societies, it seemed improbable that they were entirely culturally ordained. Not surprisingly, this one-time popular paperback is now considered to be pretty reactionary by radical thinkers.

The Sex role system (Chetwynd and Hartnett, 1978) reviewed several key areas of social activity including education. The chapter written by Glenys Lobban on 'The influence of the school on sex-role stereotyping', although obviously now superseded by more recent and more penetrating analyses, does provide a useful, brief overview of how girls and boys show different patterns of achievement, behaviour and self-evaluations in school as in other situations.

Rosemary Deem in her book Women and schooling, also published in 1978, provided the education world with a fascinating historical analysis followed by a strongly argued critique of contemporary practice in schools (Deem, 1978). One of her concerns was the way in which teacher behaviour helps to create or confirm stereotypical behaviour among pupils. Another theme that runs through the book is the way that economic stringency, a fact of life that has continued to dominate educational discussion, may greatly hinder innovations likely to amend people's attitudes and lifestyles. I have to agree with her that differentiation on grounds of sex is so often based on unequal allocation and distribution of learning resources. Shortage of funding may not only mean the continued use of sexist teaching materials, it may also prevent boys and girls from making non-traditional choices of subject because not enough teachers or facilities are available. To this I would add that when job opportunities are restricted the temptation is for parents and teachers to adopt a 'play safe' stance vis à vis career advice, however misguided this may be for the children's future.

The United States

If I were to single out one book that provides a good introduction to the North American scene in the late seventies, it would have to be Sex equity in education (Stockard et al, 1980). Written by a team of lecturers at the Center for Education Policy and Management at the University of Oregon, this was intended as a basic text on sex roles in education. It was also offered as relevant reading matter on initial and in-service education courses. Hence the emphasis is on change; the possibilities for change, the context of change in social and political processes. The main appendix provides a whole programme of exercises based on experiential learning about sex roles which could be adapted to suit the British educational context.

Four years earlier another American publication, Undoing sex stereotypes (Guttentag and Bray, 1976), had described non-sexist intervention projects and how whole-school policies can induce attitude change among staff. Although aimed at teachers in the States from 'Kindergarten through Junior High School', it contains some positive, adaptable strategies for teachers anywhere. I find it hard to believe that the American education system had already evolved to the point where the authors could say, with some conviction, in their introduction:

'Sexism in the classroom has become an old-fashioned and unpopular characteristic of the education process' (p5).

However, ten years later I do believe that some British schools still have a long way to go before sexist practices are acknowledged, let alone eliminated.

Feminist perspectives

Inevitably, it is the radical wing of the Women's Movement that has regularly fuelled the debate on sexism in education. Sara Delamont advised the reader early in the introduction to her Sex roles and the school (Delamont, 1980):

'The theory underlying the book is sociological but it is a critical, feminist sociology' (p5).

Her chapter on the 'Adolescent in school' makes salutory reading for any secondary school teacher. Dale Spender is another academic who has made very important contributions to the discussions. Her Invisible women: the schooling scandal (Spender, 1982) is as provocative as its title. This book, written with feminist fire and conviction, catalogues the way society through its institutions, particularly education, presents a one-sided view of the world - that is, a male perception. No-one is spared in her systematic critique of current practice, not even the author herself. In her section dealing with teacher-pupil interaction in mixed classrooms she highlights research that demonstrates the degree to which male dominance and attention seeking is rife. Most telling here is the gap between what teachers think they are doing and what they actually do. Attempting to distribute teacher attention equitably across the sexes is seemingly incredibly difficult. Even when she monitored her own teaching she only managed a maximum of 42% of lesson time interacting with girls. Her lessons were science lessons, but recent research at the School of Education at the University of Bath would suggest that the same male domination occurs in foreign language lessons too. (Some further details are provided in Chapter 4.)

Another researcher who has made a study of what she calls 'sexual divisions in the classroom' is Michelle Stanworth. In Gender and schooling (Stanworth, 1983) she reported on research into classroom interaction in the further education sector. Her observation ground was the relatively neutral territory of mixed 'A' level humanities classes. Even here it was noticed that fairly subtle aspects of classroom encounters continued to generate a sexual hierarchy of worth in which men emerged as the 'naturally dominant sex' (p23). Ms Stanworth also has a lot to say about pupils' awareness of the gender of their teachers and the possible effect this may have on their self-image and success in school, points that will be considered further in Chapter 4.

International studies

For readers interested in gaining an international perspective of the research and practice across the world two titles are proposed. First there is the European dimension gained by reading the published report of the Education Research workshop organised by the Council of Europe and held at Hønefoss, Norway, in May 1981. Sex stereotyping in schools (Council of Europe, 1982) reports on this phenomenon in ten countries and focusses mostly on teacher-pupil interactions and teaching materials. Alison Kelly's summary report which occupies the first twenty pages of the proceedings highlights the changes that participants felt were urgently needed to reduce sex stereotyping. For once, some attention is directed at changing boys' attitudes as well as girls'.

Margaret Sutherland's Sex bias in education (Sutherland, 1981) also provides a review, albeit somewhat general, of international studies in a chapter on other educational systems. She too points to the fact that many boys accept sex-role-indicated subjects and those who have an interest in art or music (to which I might add modern languages) may feel inhibited about displaying their interests overtly. They may adopt a contradictory posture to avoid being labelled in what they see as an unfavourable way. This brings us neatly back to the question of the labels pupils and teachers consciously or unconsciously give to subjects and activities in school.

The curriculum - overt and covert

Curriculum studies is a relatively new pursuit of education academics. The way the school curriculum is organised and presented is the main focus of their attention. But this academic science has provided additional insights into the subtle and various ways schools communicate values and assumptions to those working in their establishments (i.e. both pupils and teachers). The covert or hidden curriculum has been described by Davies and Meighan as

'those concepts of learning in schools that are unofficial or unintentional or undeclared consequences of the way in which teachers organise and execute teaching and learning'

(Davies and Meighan, 1975).

Clearly, the messages transmitted by teachers to pupils about subjects, about relative status, usefulness or difficulty - to name but a few qualities - are never value-free. Examination of curricular provision and choice has featured in most texts dealing generally with sexism, sex bias or sex discrimination.

Possibly because he is a practising headmaster, Michael Marland, as editor of the collection of essays released under the title Sex differentiation and schooling (Marland, 1983), guaranteed that his book would have a strong practical component. The contributors were asked 'to get behind the broad generalisations and to go back to basic detail' (p6), so we find sections dealing with staffing, classroom interaction, careers, etc. The hidden curriculum is studied especially as manifested through the academic consequences of teacher expectations. The overt curriculum is also treated in terms of planning, subject choice, teaching and learning materials and teaching methods. There is a chapter dealing specifically with the teaching and learning of mathematics - but hardly a mention anywhere of modern languages. To be fair, Marland recognises this in his introduction as a major gap but it is, as I warned earlier in this general literature survey, a regrettable fact that foreign language education is virtually always completely ignored or deemed worthy of only the most fleeting of references.

The same criticism cannot be levelled at Janie Whyld's Sexism in the secondary curriculum (Whyld, 1983). This is a valuable compilation of papers by different authors, each of whom analyses the ways in which sexism operates in the specialist subjects and across the curriculum. There is even a chapter on modern languages. Here Paul Hingley quotes results from the HMI 1973 survey into curricular differences for the sexes which I summarise in Chapter 2. He also reports on unpublished research that looked into pupils' attitudes and expectations about courses in the third and fourth years. Boys seemed fully aware of the problems facing them - or to be avoided by opting out - while girls, 'expecting the subject to be "difficult but stimulating"' (p100), were more prepared to face up to the difficulties and tended to attribute any subsequent loss of interest on their part to those same difficulties. Girls also gave the subject (in this case German) a much higher importance rating than boys. Hingley then concentrates on sex-stereotyping within the teaching texts available. He presents, with apposite illustrations, some positive strategies that teachers can adopt to counteract the sexist tendencies so prevalent in language teaching materials.

This is a useful chapter in a book that does not stop at description. It also proposes courses of action for teachers to counteract sexism in school policies and organisation. In her final chapter entitled 'More than one way forward' the editor casts her net wider to demonstrate how

'all concerned people, teachers, parents and pupils, can work against sexism, not as specialists but as people committed to achieving a non-sexist education' (Whyld, 1983, p295).

The tide of opinion is changing. It is no longer such a rare event, for example, to find men writing on the topic. A triumvirate consisting of John Pratt, John Bloomfield and Clive Seale carried out fairly extensive research into curricular differences in secondary schools and published the results in <u>Option choices: a question of equal opportunity</u> (Pratt, Bloomfield and Seale, 1984). The study, which was carried out five years after the Sex Discrimination Act, was intended amongst other things to monitor 'the extent to which the Act is being implemented, both in letter and spirit, and the effect it is having on secondary schools' (p1). Another vitally important goal was to 'identify and assess the practical problems which it is said preclude a free choice of curricular options by both sexes, and to examine possible solutions' (p2).

This is essential reading for anyone with an interest in option schemes – and that must mean most foreign language teachers. One of their somewhat depressing conclusions was that while the pattern of provision had changed by 1980-81, the trends in pupil choices had not altered significantly in the five years since the Act. More girls than boys were still taking subjects such as biology and languages while more boys than girls were opting for physical sciences and technical subjects. The book also investigated school policy – or lack of it – relating to sex equality of opportunity. Very few schools were observed as actively encouraging pupils to make non-traditional choices. Their survey of pupil attitudes was revealing, too. Pupil presuppositions about jobs, careers, personal qualities and activities also reflected sex-stereotypical opinions.

The Equal Opportunities Commission (EOC)

The research carried out by J Pratt and associates was supported by the EOC. This agency was set up in 1975 with the specific task of fighting sex discrimination in society. There is, naturally, a keen interest among the ranks of its members in educational manifestations of discrimination, whether obvious – as in the much publicised cases of equality of curricular choice involving e.g. girls' chances of playing football – or indirect occurrences which, many would claim, pervade secondary school practices. Several of the EOC publications are listed in the bibliography to this Guide. Particular mention could be made here of the final report of a joint action research project between the EOC and Clwyd Educational Authority. This was published in 1983 under the title: <u>Equal opportunities and the secondary school curriculum</u> (Clwyd County Council, 1983). Thirty-four schools were involved with three of them coming in for microscopic analysis. There is a useful list of recommendations directed at the LEA in question but no doubt applicable to most education authorities in the country.

Another document worthy of note is the conference report Equal
opportunities - what's in it for boys? (EOC, 1983). The conference,
held in London in November 1982, was called in order

> 'to assist in the reorientating of boys' education towards a
> less stereotyped image of their potential' (p6).

It is perhaps time that the term equal opportunities, which has come
to be associated almost exclusively with girls' and women's
education, is redefined more accurately to reflect also the needs of
male participants in the education process. Men have much to learn
about sexism and boys are, in my view, greatly disadvantaged in
certain areas of the curriculum. Once more, however, we note that
the conference overlooked modern languages, although there was a
workshop on boys' underachievement in English.

An afterthought

And yet, on reflection, the course organisers of the ILEA conference
were probably wise to tackle the broader issues, to concentrate on
gender roles as opposed to delving yet again into provision and performance in the subject specialisms. I am convinced that the key to
gender differences in school achievement and behaviour patterns lies
in pupils' definitions of gender roles. The extent to which these
roles are reinforced or denied by the organisation, provision and
processes of learning in each subject must affect boys' and girls'
opinions of them.

In the words of Jean Stockard:

> 'If sex differences in academic achievement are to lessen, it
> will be necessary to alter the cultural definitions of academic
> achievement and the male self-definition which involves a cog-
> nitive need to avoid feminine roles' (p73).

This holds true for any area of the curriculum, of course, but at
the moment boys especially seem to be manifesting a strong impulse,
a compulsive need to avoid foreign language learning. Rather, they
favour subjects in which their image of what it is to be male is
strengthened.

The role expectation of boys in their future life as husbands/pro-
viders will lead them into mainly instrumental choices regarding
their subjects of study. For the young male science is made prom-
inent. The apparent applicability of sciences to everything in adult
life and their direct relevance to career orientation make them
risky subjects to avoid. The same cannot be said of languages.

It is now time to study the field of foreign language education more
closely. We must begin by cataloguing the imbalance between the
sexes at the various stages of the educational pyramid.

2

The boy-girl imbalance in languages

Public opinions

It is a feature of most national education systems that the older the students become the fewer the subjects studied and the greater the specialisation within the selected subjects. In the case of Britain, the moments of choice when specialisation occurs are obviously at the ages of 14+ (options), 16+ (examinations at the end of compulsory schooling) and 18+ (examinations designed primarily to assess suitability for entry into higher education).

In many other systems, the curriculum narrows less early in a child's life and the opportunity to choose not to study a foreign language is presented only quite late, if at all. Most other European countries have decided in favour of some degree of compulsory language education in the mother tongue and foreign language throughout schooling until pupils begin to seek employment or entry into further or higher education sectors. Over twenty years ago some of us can remember reading the veiled warnings of the influential Newsom report:

> 'Europe as a whole is ahead of this country in including a foreign language, and often two, in the general education of a much larger proportion of its citizens. Humanly and economically speaking, insularity is behind the times.'

> (Newsom Report, 1963, p163)

In France, for example, the Baccalauréat du 2ième Degré since 1983 has demanded in all of its series an oral test in a foreign language. In Britain, on the other hand, the opportunities for early specialisation abound and with them comes the chance to abandon the study of a foreign language. Regrettably, those who have cast aside languages too soon have very little chance of returning to them or tackling new ones later on because of the way sixth form and higher education courses are currently organised.

Consequently there are numerous 'failed' linguists around the country. Evidence of successful foreign language learning is singularly lacking in society as a whole. P G Wodehouse's description has an authentic ring about it even today:

> 'Into the face of the young man who sat at the terrace of the

18

Hotel Magnifique at Cannes had crept a look of furtive shame, the shifty, hangdog look which announces that an Englishman is about to talk French.'

(from <u>The luck of the Bodkins</u>, 1958)

I suspect there are many similar events observable today.

As a nation we are quite happy to accept the status of English as a world language. Indeed, we appear to promote it by expecting foreign politicians and industrialists to use it when interviewed by British reporters abroad. Either that or we ungraciously phase out their own language as quickly as possible to replace it with an English 'voice over'. In international trade, the warnings of the British Overseas Trade Board in 1979 seem to have gone largely unheeded, viz:

'In many overseas markets British companies cannot expect to compete effectively without a knowledge of the local language .... Very few firms are making adequate use of the language training facilities already available .... Industry and commerce should adopt a more positive attitude towards foreign language skills....' (BOTB, 1979, p1)

On a purely social level, we were reminded a few years ago by our European Commissioner Christopher Tugendhat that it is gauche and ill-mannered to expect everyone else to speak one's own language without ever reciprocating.

Surely, the need for salespeople and industrialists competent in a number of languages and for linguists equipped with ancillary technical, commercial, managerial or marketing skills is not likely to diminish. The business world, however, still tends to neglect potential acquired at school level, preferring to rely largely on private organisations to provide language tuition for their personnel.

*   *   *

When the Egyptians built a pyramid, they started at the bottom. An educational pyramid, however, is best begun at the top, especially if the pyramidal design is intended to symbolise levels of involvement and success in foreign language learning. The base and lower levels will represent the years of compulsory schooling and the point will refer to the general public's knowledge of and regard for foreign languages.

So let's get to the point ....

Adult education

Many adults acquire a thirst for foreign language learning at some stage of their life after school. What had seemed an unnecessary imposition of foreign culture now takes on meaning and relevance as the opportunities for foreign travel increase. Adult classes in FE colleges and adult education centres up and down the country attract every year thousands of mature students anxious to acquire basic skills or greater proficiency in foreign languages ranging, alphabetically at least, from Arabic to Yiddish. The greatest proportion of these students claim to be beginners in the language for which they enrol. Closer examination of their 'credentials' might suggest, however, that there are many for whom the French or German lessons at school were less than totally rewarding. Or they may confess to having started learning but then having excluded languages entirely from their curriculum in favour of other subjects.

We begin our examination of the extent of the sex imbalance here, with mature students. It is not easy to gain an accurate picture of the numbers of adult foreign language learners. Nevertheless, if sales of BBC language courses are anything to go by, a substantial minority tune in regularly to the radio and TV series produced by the Continuing Education Department. Most of these would be learning in the privacy of their own home, but quite a number prefer to attach themselves to a college or adult education centre running formal language classes.

A recent survey conducted by the Language Centre at Brighton Polytechnic (Handley, 1984) provided some indication of the population involved. The information was gathered in 1983–84 from 380 centres offering 4719 classes in modern languages to 64,529 adult learners. With over 60% of the nation's centres responding to the questionnaire, the pattern of provision which emerged can be said to be reasonably representative. The bulk of the students (78%) were between the ages of 21 and 59, but in some areas the number of retired people was considerable. The overall sex ratio was 63% female and 37% male. The peak of our pyramid is thus in place:

Fig 1: <u>Sex ratio of adult learners of foreign languages</u>

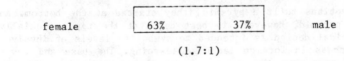

female 63% 37% male

(1.7:1)

No breakdown by sex was provided for each language taught but the ratio of nearly 2:1 is, I suspect, an accurate reflection of classes in most languages.

The teaching profession

Recognising the powerful image that teachers can present of their subject, it is argued by those anxious to encourage more girls to continue with science subjects that girls need to see more women successfully following careers in science. Especially as far as schools are concerned, the more women physics and chemistry teachers there are, the better. To what extent this same argument would apply to boys and modern languages is open to question. The predominance of women teachers in language departments is, after all, part of a wider sex-stereotyping of roles which is bound to influence a child's view of the world. The fact that so many heads of department are male is another dimension of that reality. I say 'predominance' of women language teachers based on my personal observations of the many schools I visit in the course of teaching practice supervision; but what do the official statistics tell us?

Table 1 confirms that in languages, women are in the majority. A comparison between figures for 1978 and 1983 also suggests that, if anything, the gap is widening between the sexes.

Table 1: Full-time teachers in maintained schools. All with degrees which include named subject: French at March 31st 1983 (figures for 1978 in brackets).

	Female	%	Male	%	Total
Primary	982	79.3	256	20.7	1238
	(1110)	77.2	(328)	22.8	(1438)
Secondary	6983	59.1	4821	40.8	11804
	(6402)	55.6	(5118)	44.4	(11520)
Total	7965	61.1	5086	38.9	13051
	(7512)	58.0	(5446)	42.0	(12958)

SOURCE: Statistics of Education: Teachers in Service, DES 1983

Information relating to modern languages other than French is grouped together for all languages, making the presentation of separate tables for German, Spanish, etc impossible. In this grouping of languages, however, the distribution of the sexes is much more even. There are, indeed, probably more male teachers of German, although, as we shall see in a moment, the picture at undergraduate level is not so different from that of French.

21

Table 2: Full-time teachers in maintained schools. All with degrees which include named subject: Modern languages other than French at March 31st 1983 (figures for 1978 in brackets).

	Female	%	Male	%	Total
Primary	802	72.7	301	27.3	1103
	(693)	68.5	(318)	31.5	(1011)
Secondary	4803	51.7	4489	48.3	9292
	(3851)	46.0	(4528)	54.0	(8379)
Total	5605	53.9	4790	46.1	10395
	(4544)	48.4	(4846)	51.6	(9390)

SOURCE: Statistics of Education: Teachers in Service, DES 1983.

It should be noted that in 1978 male teachers of languages other than French outnumbered female teachers while five years later the situation is reversed.

So the second set of layers of our pyramid – working downwards – is now complete with the following approximations.

Fig 2: Sex ratio of teachers of French

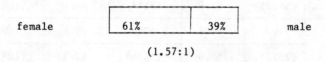

female   61%   39%   male

(1.57:1)

Fig 3: Sex ratio of teachers of modern languages other than French

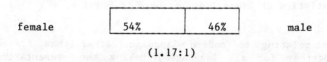

female   54%   46%   male

(1.17:1)

New entrants to the teaching profession

Just over 8000 people were accepted to follow Postgraduate Certificate in Education (PGCE) courses during the academic year 1984-85.

Of these, 4545 pursued the intitial teacher training course in University Departments of Education (UDEs) and 3578 went to public sector institutions, polytechnics or colleges of higher ecucation. Recruitment for BEd courses in modern languages ceased in 1983. In 1984, of those still in the system men were greatly outnumbered by women, in fact by 1:10.5.

Table 3: Students completing BEd courses (Modern languages)

1984 BEd Primary and secondary All languages	Female	%	Male	%	Total
	148	91.4	14	8.6	162

SOURCE: Central Register and Clearing House, Graduate Teacher Training Registry (GTTR), 1985.

The normal initial training language teachers now receive is on the PGCE course. 1984 saw 889 students accepted with languages as principal method subjects. Details are provided in the tables below. The numbers refer to all languages other than English. Any further categorisation by individual language is rendered impossible because in many institutions all language students follow a common programme of work.

Table 4: UDEs: PGCE foreign languages

Year of entry	Female	%	Male	%	Total
1982	580	73.9	205	26.1	785
1983	529	74.0	186	26.0	715
1984	474	69.4	209	30.6	683

SOURCE: Graduate Teacher Training Registry, 1985.

Table 5: Public sector institutions: PGCE foreign languages

Year of entry	Female	%	Male	%	Total
1982	264	77.4	77	22.6	341
1983	161	70.0	69	30.0	230
1984	188	76.4	58	23.6	246

SOURCE: Graduate Teacher Training Registry, 1985.

Table 6: **All teacher training institutions: PGCE foreign languages**

Year of entry	Female	%	Male	%	Total
1982	844	75.0	282	25.0	1126
1983	690	73.0	255	27.0	945
1984	662	71.3	267	28.7	929

SOURCE: Graduate Teacher Training Registry, 1985

Falling rolls in schools and economic cuts are having a real effect in reducing the teaching staff. Even over a three-year span the trend is quite noticeable with 200 fewer trained language teachers considering joining the profession. I say 'considering' for some will choose alternative careers at the end of their training year. Some, indeed, will never make it to the end of the year! The reduction in numbers is actually more pronounced among women students than men. The pattern of entry perpetuates, if not increases, the sex imbalance which many teachers assume exists among qualified teaching staff. On the pyramid this would slot in as follows.

Fig 4: **Sex ratio of language teachers in training**

female	73.2%	26.8%	male

(2.7:1)

Research and higher degree courses

There is one notable exception to the pattern being established by this analysis of available statistics. In the field of higher degree work women are in the minority when all combinations of language (including English), literature and area studies are taken into account.

Table 7: **Full-time students at postgraduate level in all languages (including English)**
Research and taught courses at 31 December 1983

	Female				Male				
All langu-ages	Research	Taught	Total	%	Research	Taught	Total	%	Over-all total
	612	461	1073	44.2	827	527	1354	55.8	2427

SOURCE: Universities Statistical Records, 1984

24

In the most commonly taught foreign languages, the figures are more evenly balanced but, given the imbalance at first degree level, a far larger percentage of men than women currently seem to benefit from research studentships or bursaries.

Table 8: Full-time students at postgraduate level in three modern languages at 31 December 1983

	Female				Male				Over-all total
	Research	Taught	Total	%	Research	Taught	Total	%	
French lang/ studies	58	10	68	54.4	53	4	57	45.6	125
German lang/ studies	31	8	39	43.3	44	7	51	56.7	90
Spanish lang/ studies	23	10	33	53.2	18	˙11	29	46.8	62
Total 3 langu-ages	112	28	140	50.5	115	22	137	49.5	277

SOURCE: Universities Statistical Records, 1984

The male preference for German is noticeable here but generally speaking the figures provide a remarkable example of equilibrium in what is becoming a rather lop-sided pyramid.

Fig 5: Sex ratio of research and higher degree students in modern languages

female | 50.5% | 49.5% | male

First degree courses

The next stage to be analysed must obviously be the undergraduate level. The Universities' Statistical Record provides very detailed information on undergraduate course entry and completion. The most recent complete picture obtainable, however, relates to 1982. The usual length of degree courses for foreign languages is four years, including a year spent abroad, but there are three and even five year courses operating too. Table 9 presents the details for the academic year 1982/83. A comparison can be made with the situation four years earlier by studying the figures in brackets. It is worth recording here two aspects arising out of this comparison.

a) There is an overall increase in the number of undergraduates enrolled for foreign language courses, exactly 1060 as it happens. This is in line with birthrate curves and the increase overall in the numbers of students in higher education. But 1982/83 marked the high point; subsequent years will show a decline.

b) Whereas, with the exception of Russian, the number of women specialising in languages increased over the four year span, the number of men has reduced in all languages listed. The gap is widening.

Table 9: Full-time and sandwich undergraduates in British universities on 3,4 and 5 year courses to first degree/diploma in languages (1982/83)
(1978 figures in brackets)

	Women	%	(Nos in 1978)	Men	%	(Nos in 1978)	Total	(Total 1978)
French	3241	80.2	(3136)	799	19.8	(851)	4040	(3987)
French/ German	1576	72.9	(1181)	585	27.1	(583)	2161	(1764)
German	1354	71.8	(1111)	533	28.2	(542)	1887	(1653)
Hispanic langs	575	73.0	(542)	213	27.0	(275)	788	(817)
Russian	245	61.6	(261)	153	38.4	(176)	398	(437)
Other West European langs	2351	78.0	(1902)	663	22.0	(668)	3014	(2570)
Total	9342	76.0	(8133)	2946	24.0	(3095)	2288	(11228)

SOURCE: Universities Statistical Records, 1984

Since it is anticipated that most readers of this Guide will be practising schoolteachers, it seems appropriate to compile another set of data relating specifically to the main foreign languages taught in British schools. So, with apologies to Italianists and all those teachers of our other community languages (for whom no separate details are provided), the totals for degree courses in French, German, Spanish and Russian will be as follows.

Table 10: Undergraduates in British universities on 3, 4 and 5 year
          courses to first degree in main languages taught in
          school (1982-83)
          (1978 figures in brackets)

Female	%	(1978)	Male	%	(1978)	Total	(1978)
6971	75.3	(6231)	2283	24.7	(2427)	9254	(8658)

SOURCE: Universities Statistical Records, 1984

This combination provides us with an additional building block for
our pyramid in which the female bias is again much in evidence. The
gap has widened here, too, over four years with 144 fewer men on
course for a modern language degree but 740 more women.

Fig 6: Sex ratio of undergraduate foreign language students

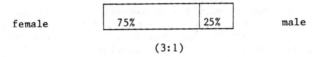

female   75%   25%   male

(3:1)

Examinations at 18+

The number of young people studying a foreign language in the sixth
form represents a small proportion of the examinable population at
that level. Most telling is a graphic representation of the proportion of school leavers attempting examinations in modern languages
at the beginning, and at the end of the seventies.

Fig 7: 'A' level entries (England and Wales): French

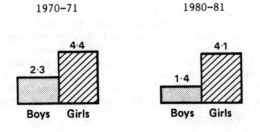

1970-71   1980-81

2·3   4·4   1·4   4·1

Boys Girls   Boys Girls

Fig 8:   'A' level entries (England and Wales)
         other modern languages

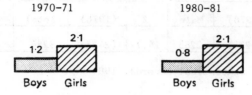

        1970-71   1980-81

One local survey I recently conducted in 42 mixed comprehensive
schools produced only 321 'A' level French students in both years of
the sixth form. There were 287 girls to 34 boys, a ratio of 8.4:1.
This imbalance is more pronounced than the national average and, not
surprisingly, alarmed teachers in the schools concerned.

Statistics of examination entries and results are notoriously difficult to compile for the amateur researcher. Fortunately, however,
in recent Inspection Reports, Her Majesty's Inspectorate (HMI) has
wisely taken the step of including statistical appendices. We
reprint some of the details provided in these, for the next layer of
our pyramid depends on them. Table 11 shows total entries and the
number of passes for each sex over a four year period. Two things
should be borne in mind while studying these figures: the figures
may appear relatively steady from year to year, but the numbers of
pupils staying on after the age of 16 have increased; the ratio of
success girls to boys has increased noticeably even in this span of
time. For example, in 1979 for French the ratio was 1.78:1, for
German 1.99:1, and in Spanish 2.3:1. In 1983, the same calculation
produces French 2.71:1, German 2.39:1, and Spanish 2.65:1.

It must be noted that Table 11 (see facing page) includes candidates
from further education colleges and overseas candidates. This table
also permits us to monitor the trends over the period illustrated.
What is especially noticeable is the decline in the number of boys
studying French. It is worth recording that in 1968, 7169 boys
passed 'A' level French. The figures for 1983 show an improvement (a
hiccup in the birthrate?), but the trend is still downwards and the
gap between the sexes widens each year. A glance at another set of
statistics for the year 1981-82 referring uniquely to state maintained schools (Table 12) will reveal a greater distance between the
sexes at this level. Readers will derive their own conclusions from
these figures.

28

Table 11   GCE 'A' level results by subject 1979-83

ENGLISH BOARDS ONLY

SUBJECTS	1979			1980			1981			1982			1983		
	PASSES		ENTRIES	PASSES		ENTRIES	PASSES		ENTRIES	PASSES		ENTRIES	PASSES		ENTRIES
	M	F	TOTAL	M	F	TOTAL	M	F	TOTAL	M	F	TOTAL	M	F	TOTAL
FRENCH	6,854	12,259	26,018	5,107	12,617	24,262	5,131	12,911	24,847	4,912	13,496	25,145	5,546	15,032	25,169
GERMAN	2,174	4,325	8,182	2,128	4,419	8,274	2,134	4,772	8,606	2,067	5,101	8,900	2,330	5,566	9,102
SPANISH	616	1,421	2,611	562	1,486	2,718	597	1,579	2,823	622	1,640	2,934	684	1,812	2,930
ITALIAN	192	402	806	162	459	818	118	392	635	160	433	744	180	492	741
RUSSIAN	160	171	396	135	178	372	133	188	372	133	186	377	119	173	313
OTHER MODERN LANGUAGES	385	367	926	449	446	1,110	415	407	1,061	432	468	1,078	629	538	1,326

Source: (HMI, 1985b)

29

Table 12: **Entries in modern languages at GCE 'A' level – maintained schools: school leavers 1981–82**

	BOYS	GIRLS	TOTAL
FRENCH	3,220 (21.3%) Ratio of Boys to Girls 1:3.7	11,910 (78.7%)	15,130 (100%)
GERMAN	1,266 (22.1%) Ratio 1:3.5	4,430 (77.9%)	5,690 (100%)
ITALIAN	40 (18.2%) Ratio 1:4.5	180 (81.8%)	220 (100%)
RUSSIAN	50 (25%) Ratio 1:3	150 (75%)	200 (100%)
SPANISH	350 (19.9%) Ratio 1:4	1,410 (80.1%)	1,760 (100%)
TOTAL FRENCH AND OTHER MODERN LANGU-AGES (some not specified)	5,070 (21.8%) Ratio 1:3.6	18,200 (78%)	23,280 (100%)

SOURCE: (HMI, 1985a)

On average, therefore, there are nearly four girls to every one boy pursuing an Advanced level language course. Pass rates differ from language to language, from sector to sector and, obviously, from school to school, but based on 1983 our sex ratio of success for the commonly taught languages would be:

Fig 9: Sex ratio of examination passes at 18+

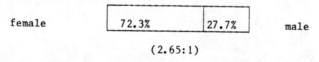

female   72.3%   27.7%   male

(2.65:1)

Examinations at 16+

Whereas the proportion of modern language students at 'A' level had declined between 1970 and 1980, the population taking language exams at the end of compulsory schooling had increased.

Percentage of school leavers in England and Wales
attempting examinations in modern languages at 16+

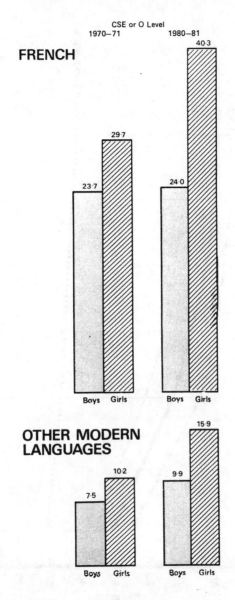

CSE or O Level
1970—71   1980—81

FRENCH

40·3

29·7

23·7   24·0

Boys   Girls   Boys   Girls

OTHER MODERN
LANGUAGES

15·9

10·2   9·9

7·5

Boys   Girls   Boys   Girls

SOURCE: (DES, 1983)

31

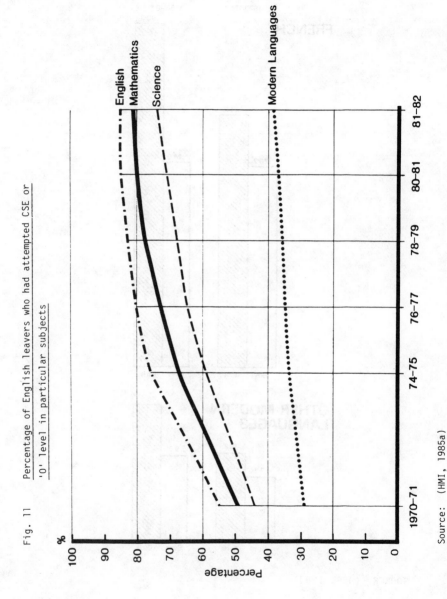

Fig. 11 Percentage of English leavers who had attempted CSE or 'O' level in particular subjects

English
Mathematics
Science
Modern Languages

Percentage

100
90
80
70
60
50
40
30
20
10
0

1970-71   74-75   76-77   78-79   80-81   81-82

Source: (HMI, 1985a)

32

The bar graphs which form Fig 10 give an impression of progress and growth. However, to put the increases into perspective, we need to compare the rate of increase in languages with that in other subjects as the exam population has itself increased over the decade (see Fig 11). In real terms, the entries in languages have not kept pace with the other subjects even though more pupils have been given access to foreign language learning following reorganisation along comprehensive lines.

There are differences in entry figures for the various languages and in the two examinations at this level, CSE and 'O' level. It is impossible to provide all the details here. A study of the case of French, however, reveals a trend which is striking in its consistency. CSE entries have continued to increase over the years. Has 'O' level become more difficult or were the standards set years ago before comprehensive schools were created based on too high expectations of pupil performance in English and the foreign language? Whatever the case, while CSE continues to attract more candidates, the gap between the sexes is widening here too.

Fig 12: <u>CSE French entries 1967-83</u>

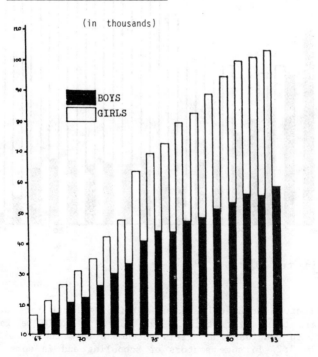

Source: (O'Brien, 1985)

33

At 'O' level the decline in the numbers of boys is most marked and since the beginning of the eighties both sexes seem to be turning away increasingly from French.

Fig 13:   'O' level French entries 1966-83

(in thousands)

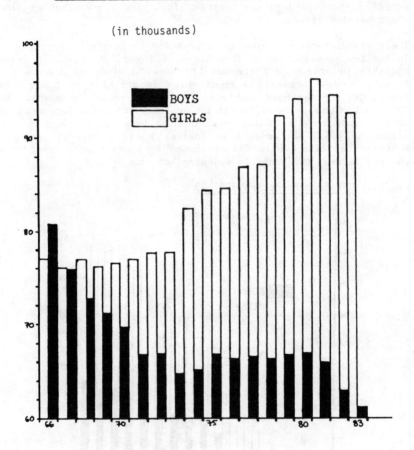

Source: (O'Brien, 1985)

To construct an accurately measured building block for our pyramid out of all these statistics is not easy. It would be fair, even generous, to conclude that girls outnumber boys in 16+ examination entries by 3:2. In some sectors of schooling and in some languages it is probably nearer 3:1.

Fig 14:   Sex ratio 16+ examinations

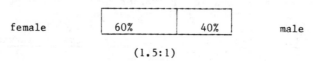

```
female          |   60%   |   40%   |          male
```
(1.5:1)

Choices at the option stage

The presence of a foreign language in the core curriculum for all
pupils 11-16 would inevitably reduce the discrepancy between male
and female candidature at examinations at age 16+. But such an innovation in curricular provision, in the words of HMI 'can be envis-
aged only as a long-term goal' (HMI, 1985a, p21). Besides, the
teaching profession is divided on the issue with many language
teachers still regarding such a change as an undesirable development.

Revisions in the examination syllabuses and the introduction of a
single system for all pupils are seen as positive initiatives by
some, if not all teachers in the system. At present, any review of
national or regional examination results will tend only to add to
the aura of femininity surrounding languages. We should not need
reminding that results in themselves do not add anything to our
understanding of the process of language learning, nor the influences that are brought to bear on young people at the decisive moment
of choice, at the option stage. The results should not be used to
support any claim that languages are 'girls' subjects' and inherent-
ly feminine. They merely show that more boys than girls choose not
to do languages for reasons that may have nothing to do with a perception of the subject as feminine or otherwise on the part of the
pupils.

The results of decisions at the option stage in mixed schools produce fourth and fifth year classes where boys are increasingly unlikely to feature. Some ten years ago a survey by HMI of 10% of
maintained schools revealed pretty starkly the unpopularity of
languages especially as far as the boys were concerned. In the 447
survey schools the take-up for French was 24% boys, 40% girls. In
German it was 5% boys, 8% girls. A similar survey conducted today
would, I suspect, produce similar results. Indeed, the pattern of
examination entries charted in the preceding section of this chapter
would suggest even less favourable figures and a widening gap.

With over 90% of pupils now being given the chance to study a language in the early years of secondary school, a national average of
33-35% uptake at the option stage must be viewed as disappointing.

Even when pupils have made their choices it appears that satisfaction is not guaranteed. A Schools Council exploratory study of option choices in ten schools in 1982 produced a gloomy picture for language teachers in those schools and elsewhere.

Table 13: Satisfaction with specific options: overall ranking by 4th and 5th formers in 10 schools

Relative satisfaction (1 = most satisfaction, 15 = least satisfaction)	Option
1	Woodwork
2	Office practice/typing/shorthand
3	Metalwork
4	Home economics
5 =	Art
5 =	Biology
7	Physics
8	Commerce
9	Geography
10	Religious education
11	History
12	German
13	Chemistry
14	Technical drawing
15	French

SOURCE: Options for the Fourth, Schools Council (1982)

In the HMI survey which resulted in the publication Boys and modern languages in 1985 (HMI, 1985a), 32 schools were involved. The original aim had been to identify schools where the number of boys choosing to take one or more modern language exceeded 50% of the total take up. In fifteen of the main sample of schools selected by Inspectors the take-up rate did exceed 50%. However, it must be borne in mind that in six of these a language was a core curriculum subject and in another seven the options scheme operating actively encouraged pupils to continue with a language or made it very difficult to avoid languages. Only two of the schools then operated the more usual free choice option system. In no school did the boys actually outnumber the girls. In all, the survey looked at eight schools with open or free choice as far as modern languages were concerned. Some of these schools 'qualified' for inclusion in the survey because the combined percentage uptake for the sexes was boosted well above 50% by the girls alone. In one school, the gap between the sexes was significantly worse than usual: 77.1% of all pupils continued with a language but this was composed of 16.0% boys – 61.1% girls. This is probably more in line with the experience of the majority of language teachers in mixed schools.

It is certainly becoming more difficult to maintain pupils' initial enthusiasm for foreign language learning and to attract pupils of both sexes on to examination courses in years four and five. In a foreign language research project at the School of Education of the University of Bath (hereafter called the University of Bath project), seven mixed comprehensive schools with good records of attracting 'large' numbers of pupils of French and German into the fourth year were the subject of a detailed analysis of option choices during 1985. (For an outline of the University of Bath project and some preliminary results see Powell and Batters, 1985.) In one of the schools some foreign language study formed part of the core curriculum in the last two years of compulsory schooling. In another school German was offered as first foreign language; two other schools gave German equal first foreign language status with French by offering the subject to half the first year intake each year. It is difficult to say whether these less usual patterns of provision affected the outcome of the options process at the end of the third year. Perhaps no direct link between organisation and pupils' choice of examination courses should be made. However, the proportion of pupils electing to take a foreign language – 47% of the school population involved – is well above the national average at around 33%. The distribution by sex within this 47% worked out at 59.2% female as opposed to 40.8% male, a ratio of 1.45:1. Nationally the gap between the sexes is marginally wider at approximately 62% female to 38% male (1.64:1). Apparently then, even when schools devise teaching arrangements that accentuate languages other than French within the curriculum, radical shifts in patterns of pupil choices are not automatically guaranteed. Boys and girls tend to continue to make conventional selections.

As we near the base of the educational pyramid, therefore, we see that the ratio of girls to boys for courses of further study in years four and five is, by and large, set after only two or three years of exposure to foreign language teaching.

Fig 15:   Sex ratio at 14+: the option stage

female | 62% | 38% | male

(1.63:1)

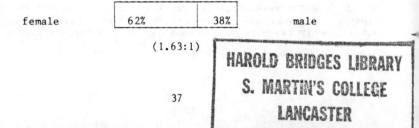

37

The first three years of foreign language learning

We have now reached what we may call the foundations of our pyramid. There is, indeed, one further feature of the sex imbalance, not to say segregation, that occurs even earlier than the option stage.

Research has shown, and common sense told us already, that pupils generally opt for subjects in which they feel they have a reasonable chance of success. Pupils are quick to evaluate their own position within the school hierarchy where academic success is the prize. British teachers of foreign languages have, generally speaking, rejected the notion of mixed-ability teaching for other than the very early stages of learning. They prefer to set pupils according to proven or assumed linguistic ability. I say 'assumed' because in some schools setting can take place as early as half-term in the first term of the first year. It has been my view for a long time that many able boys fail to take languages seriously or appear to be performing less well than girls because they find themsleves relegated too early to ability sets lower than is appropriate. Consequently, those pupils in the school who appear to be linguistically gifted tend to be girls. There is little chance of redressing the balance between boys and girls in the upper school if the imbalance has already been created and fixed during, or at the end of, the first year.

In an attempt to determine the extent to which pupils were split by sex at the same time as they were setted by ability, I conducted, in 1983, a survey of mixed comprehensive schools in one local authority. To speak of segregation would be to create the idea that there was a conscious choice on the part of the staff, usually heads of department, who drew up the rolls for the setted classes, to separate the sexes. On the contrary, I have met many teachers, male and female, who make a conscious effort to keep the sets equally balanced between the sexes. This usually means creating a top band of broader ability in order to include those boys who would otherwise be placed in the second or third sets. Generally, however, reorganising pupil groupings after mixed ability classes or broad bands does result in many more girls than boys being placed in top sets and, conversely, a preponderance of boys in the bottom sets. It is not my purpose here to argue for or against policies of positive discrimination for one sex or the other. In this chapter I am more concerned to illustrate the extent of the phenomenon of sex imbalance in foreign language classes. I do, however, question the wisdom of a policy of setting pupils so early after their initial encounter with a foreign language if so marked an imbalance in the allocation of places as shown in Table 14 is created. An extreme, but by no means isolated, case was that where one school reorganised classes into sets at Christmas time in the first year and, come January, only two boys were deemed worthy of a top set place.

38

Table 14:   Distribution of the sexes in top sets* for French in 42
            mixed comprehensive schools after year 1

	Girls	%	Boys	%
Year 2	936	66.0	482	34.0
Year 3	964	63.4	556	36.6

*Some schools operated schemes with two parallel top sets drawn from
broader bands of ability.

The final phase of pyramid building, therefore, has at last been
reached with the base looking distinctly similar to the layers upon
which it is constructed.

Fig 16:   Sex ratio at 12+ following setting by ability

female | 65% | 35% | male

                        (1.85:1)

In the preceding pages, I have shown how, at various key stages in
our education system, the numbers studying foreign languages decline. The majority of those who remain in the system are female.
This is not unexpected perhaps when we realise how organisation and
provision in some schools may actually reduce the chances for equality of opportunity very early. A glance at Figure 17 (see p 40), the
complete pyramid, will show the progressive steps of our analysis.
The scale of the various layers may not reflect accurately the numbers involved, but the division of the sexes in terms of access to
and perseverence in formal language learning is quite starkly repre-
sented.

By cataloguing the numerical imbalance between the sexes I hope to
have alerted the teaching profession to the risks of perpetuating
forms of organisation and expectations that can serve only to reinforce the view that languages are more appropriate for girls than
boys. Personally, I place a high value on foreign language education
for all, for the duration of compulsory schooling. I fear a system
that permits such early specialisation.

Perhaps language teachers should now be looking forward more positively to a time when no school subject will be labelled masculine
or feminine and when it will be perfectly normal for both boys and
girls to learn a foreign language for at least five years. This,
after all, is the situation in so many other countries where, mind-

39

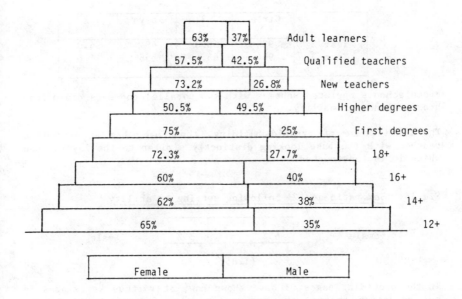

63%	37%	Adult learners
57.5%	42.5%	Qualified teachers
73.2%	26.8%	New teachers
50.5%	49.5%	Higher degrees
75%	25%	First degrees
72.3%	27.7%	18+
60%	40%	16+
62%	38%	14+
65%	35%	12+

Female	Male

ful of vocational, cultural, economic and recreational goals, teachers are encouraging pupils, irrespective of sex, to develop language skills beyond minimum survival levels.

In this chapter I have laid stress on the structure of education.
Questions still remain. Why is it that the imbalance can be created
so soon? What factors besides organisational constraints determine
an individual pupil's performance in foreign language learning? What
factors influence an individual's motivation and attitude, so
crucial to success in academic achievement? In the next chapter the
focus will be on some of the research that has considered biological, cognitive and affective variables in language learning and
the ways the sexes may differ in these.

3

Sex differences in language learning: myths and reality

So far, few people seem to have viewed the issue of sex- stereotyping in foreign languages as a problem. However, by now it must be apparent to any reader that concern is justified when the full implications of the evidence of the sex imbalance are considered. My review of the literature on the topic of gender differences and sexism in Chapter 1 yielded very few direct references to languages, apart from occasional statements about the language arts in general. Certainly there is a rich field of study awaiting researchers in the specific area of foreign-language learning. A qualification in cognitive or behavioural psychology and psycholinguistics would be desirable for potential investigators, for we really know very little about the processes of second-language learning and any differences that may exist between female and male learners at various stages of maturity.

The language of educational research is notorious for its speculative style and circumspection. Writing on this topic is no exception. Consider this example taken from the conclusion to a review article on innate sex differences in linguistic ability.

'We have seen that there <u>may</u> be sex differences in both linguistic ability and functional brain lateralization, and the two <u>may</u> be causally related. If the differences do exist, they <u>may</u> be related more to handedness than sex and <u>may</u> be influenced by hormonal activity, or correlated with age of maturity, or <u>may</u> perhaps be mostly induced by social factors.'

(G Hurst, 1982, p110. Not my emphasis)

With similar caution we embark on a brief review of research in the field.

Focus 1: Biological and cognitive differences

'It is obvious that girls are predestined for excellence in foreign languages. They have an innate capacity for language learning.'

This comment was among those I received a couple of years ago in the free response section of a questionnaire directed at modern language teachers. I had asked the question:

'In many schools, once setting occurs, fewer boys than girls find their way into the top sets for foreign languages: have you any opinions as to why this should happen?'

I believe the respondent in this case was convinced of the correctness of the view expressed. I am not sure how the judgement was arrived at, but I suspect that it had a profound influence on that teacher's expectations of pupil performance. Anyone who studies the available evidence, however, is unlikely to produce such a confident verdict. The arguments for and against the existence of predestined biological sex differences in language potential continue to emerge but, in reality, empirical data is scant and inconclusive. Besides, as yet, to the best of my knowledge, there have been no major enquiries through cognitive psychology in the field of foreign language as distinct from first language acquisition. As for connections between language acquisition and second-language learning – well, that too is another virtually uncharted sea.

I have already suggested that Maccoby and Jacklin share some responsibility for establishing the idea that girls are somehow specially endowed with superior language skills. In those test results that they examined in which girls scored higher than boys, the experiments were generally measuring mechanical aspects of speech and language – articulation, fluency, speed and accuracy of reading, and the like.

Girls aged 5–11 also seemed to be quicker at tasks involving random automatised naming of colours, objects, letters and numbers. But in other tests which might have a bearing on foreign language aptitude, e.g. comprehension, recall and vocabulary tests, boys aged 6–11 fared better (Brimer, 1969). More recent tests of recall of listening comprehension produced mixed results for boys and girls (Riding and Vincent, 1980). Boys seemed to excel when speech rates quickened but otherwise girls when not under pressure of time performed better at all ages in the 7–15 year age-span.

In these experiments, as in the vast majority of the research, there are more variations in the results within the sexes than between the sexes. Where differences do occur they are seldom statistically significant. Overall, the conclusions made by Maccoby and Jacklin which led people to believe in girls' superior verbal abilities are very questionable. Furthermore, the greater proportion of the research they analysed (62%) showed no sex differences whatsoever.

Macaulay, writing in 1978, argued that female superiority in language is a myth, and he enumerated a number of equivocal results emanating from studies in the sixties and seventies. He also pointed to variations in similar tests with children from different cultures. To claim the existence of innate sex differences, similar results should be observable across different societies and cultures, and universally acknowledged. This is most certainly not the case. Girls and boys perform differently in different countries. Macaulay also went so far as to suggest that the personal integrity of some researchers is questionable. He wrote:

'Most investigators have been so convinced of the linguistic superiority of girls that they have looked at the evidence with a rather jaundiced eye. As a result they have exaggerated reports of slight differences in favour of girls into convincing proof of female superiority.' (Macaulay, 1978, p358)

Macaulay's conclusion that 'in the present state of language assessment the only tenable position is that there is NO significant difference between the sexes in linguistic ability' (p361) has not prevented other writers from reiterating the conventional and popular wisdom; that is, perpetuating the myth of female superiority. The seemingly authoritative volume Sex-related differences in cognitive functioning (Wittig and Peterson, 1979) tends to do just this. In one chapter Waber writing on 'Variations in the maturation of cerebral cortical functions' reproduces Maccoby and Jacklin almost word for word. Bryden in a chapter on 'Sex differences in cerebral organisation' is fortunately a little more judicious when summarising:

'At present it is difficult to see any patterns emerging. Any conclusions rest on one's choice of which studies to emphasise and which to ignore.' (Wittig and Peterson, 1979, p137)

Stockard (Stockard, 1980) reminds us that results vary considerably from country to country. Reading achievement scores for the two sexes seem prone to fluctuation across the world, with many more boys frequenting remedial reading classes in Germany, Britain, Canada and the United States. International studies of foreign language achievement highlight that girls are more likely to gain high scores in some countries. A student's sex, for example, contributed considerable variance in the performance of certain language skills, listening and reading mostly, in Carroll's study of French as a foreign language in eight countries (Carroll, 1975). In the significant cases, girls were always better. Interestingly, the pattern of results demonstrated that the 'femininity' stereotype was most marked in English-speaking countries in his survey (England, Scotland, United States) but similar trends, curiously, were noted in Chile.

Klann-Delius (Klann-Delius, 1981) took up her own critical stance to judge whether a person's sex influences his or her ability to learn language. Restricting her analysis to a developmental psycholinguistic aspect, she wrote separately about the classical components of language, phonology, syntax and semantics. She also considered the acquisition of pragmatic rules and the development of communicative competence in the first language. Wisely, she considered most

claims of innate sex difference made previously to be controversial.
She concluded:

'The empirical investigations do not admit to the drawing of any
reasonable conclusion about the influence of sex on children's
language acquisition.' (p9)

She illustrated many of the methodological inadequacies that have
characterised the majority of the studies and warned of the risks in
measuring total linguistic ability from isolated features of linguistic performance. For too long, she argued, people have associated difference automatically with deficit. She urged for more
meticulous research that would bring about what she called

'a productive dismantling of the stereotype which assumes that
one sex is better than the other in linguistic matters.' (p19)

Hirst (Hirst, 1982) concentrated on brain symmetry, handedness, age
of maturity and endocrine influence - the role of hormones - in his
evaluation of research evidence. He rejects most findings as inconclusive. He then reminds readers that even when biological differences are found, even lateralisation anomalies, socialisation may well
have played a crucial role in their formation. The practice of
skills associated with assigned sex roles, he suggests, affects
cognitive as well as physical growth.

He cites Nash in Wittig (1979) who showed that reading is perceived
by children in the USA as a feminine activity, and that boys who
perceive it as more feminine are somewhat poorer readers.

Do boys and girls approach foreign-language learning with entirely
open minds? Probably not. Tenuous claims about biological differences and deficits are in themselves highly emotive and susceptible to
abuse and misuse. Far more significant are those attributes of an
individual's personality and perceptions which bear upon her or his
willingness to be educated and motivated to persevere with a learning task.

Focus 2: Affective factors

If we accepted the validity of those research studies that suggest
there _are_ differences between the sexes in terms of brain lateralisation and cognitive styles and, even at the risk of producing a
biased set of principles, deliberately rejected those in which _no_
differences were found or those which actually allowed males to
dominate, the degree of difference between the sexes is of little
import when we place it in the context of strong environmental
influence and the overwhelming effects of socialisation processes.
Even theories such as differing rates of maturity need to take
account of the possibility that the practice of skills associated

with recognisable and long-standing sex roles can actually serve to influence the development of those same skills and the cognitive functions that help to bring them about. Successful foreign language learning in the formal context of a secondary school classroom is dependent on many factors. Among the learner variables in empirical research studies of foreign language acquisition, factors such as intelligence, aptitude and memory have regularly been under consideration. Societal factors such as parental support, socio-economic grouping and teacher-pupil interaction have also, justifiably, been the subject of much debate. However, discussions on language teaching methodology have tended recently to highlight the affective variables which advance or constrain learning. Over the past ten years or so, language teachers have increasingly rejected the highly structured approaches of audio-visual or audio-lingual methods whose development was underpinned by behaviourist psychology. With the emphasis now less on formal repetition and pattern practice of grammatical and syntactical items and more on communicative goals and the comprehension of authentic language, classroom activities are now more likely to make demands on pupils' willingness to absorb the foreign culture and to identify with and emulate the speakers of the target language. It seems timely, therefore, to examine what is known as the 'affective domain' in the parlance of humanistic psychology. The focus must now be on the learner as a whole person, and primarily an emotional being.

There are various personality factors likely to influence language learning: extroversion – introversion, anxiety – confidence, empathy – ethnocentricity, perseverance – irresolution. All these and other human qualities make up a person's attitudes towards school and school subjects.

Measuring attitudes accurately is not the easiest branch of social science research. Those being surveyed usually indicate their level of agreement with a variety of statements, both positive and negative, about the subject under scrutiny by ticking appropriate boxes or ringing numbers in a series. The way the sentences are framed, the sequence in which they occur, even the format in which they are presented may influence an individual's reactions. As for the respondents themselves the way they complete the questionnaire will reflect a momentary opinion which may well be different had the document been presented the following week, the next day – even five minutes later! Also, when it comes to asking questions which isolate sex differences (however subtly) the strength of opinion which reflects same-sex, peer-group identity should not be underestimated. Some pupils may be unable to distinguish between loyalty to their own sex and their true feelings about the performance of one or other sex. It is essential, therefore, when reporting research at least to bear these factors in mind, as well as monitoring the numbers involved. Most frequently validity and reliability have to be taken on trust. It is rare to come across research, the results of which can claim to be statistically representative, to be a true reflection of the total population's views. In the field of modern languages, such large-scale research is virtually non-existent.

Links between attitudes and proficiency in language learning are well established. However, most investigations have been carried out among adult learners, students in higher education or under learning conditions that bear little resemblance to the classrooms of British secondary schools, for example in bilingual socio-cultural settings or during language immersion programmes. Certainly foreign language education in Britain does not have the support of extensive empirical research studies.

One major survey which did involve large numbers of pupils was that conducted by Clare Burstall into the teaching of French in primary schools in the late sixties and early seventies. The repercussions of that longitudinal study are only too well known to language teachers. Burstall's conclusion that

'the weight of the evidence has combined with the balance of opinion to tip the scales against a possible expansion of the teaching of French in primary schools' (Burstall, 1974, p246).

was the signal to LEAs up and down the country to phase out French in their primary schools. Criticisms were made at the time about the validity of some of the achievement tests used and the lack of consideration of factors other than achievement which ought to be taken into account when making decisions about curricula (Buckby, 1976). But what interests me here is the considerable evidence of gender differences, not just in most of the performance tests, but in attitudes to French and the French. These were already well-established by the age of eleven. In most items that monitored reactions to the language, culture and the lesson contents girls had a much more favourable attitude to learning than boys. That children's attitudes were so firmly rooted and, in the case of boys so antagonistic to French may not now appear so surprising. The association between attitudes and achievement was undeniable. Attitudes alter, of course, as one matures, but the extent to which schools can counteract prejudice which sometimes borders on xenophobia is debatable.

The primary schools' classes, if not all the secondary classes, in Burstall's survey were mixed. In the same year as the final volume of her research report was published, R R Dale produced his third volume of a detailed examination of the educational experiences of pupils in mixed and single-sex schools (Dale, 1974). French was one of the subjects singled out for special mention with regard to pupil attitudes. Girls, overall, were more favourably disposed to learn French than boys. Girls' liking for French steadily increased between the ages of 11 and 15, more in mixed than single-sex schools though. On the other hand, boys in boys' schools showed an appreciably greater interest in French than those in mixed schools and at age 15 this difference was statistically significant for all social classes.

More specifically interested in differences between mixed and single-sex schools as they affect uptake in French, Beswick (Beswick, 1976) monitored two cohorts of pupils in seven boys' schools and eight mixed schools in order to ascertain the polarisation of pupils' attitudes and achievements. He concluded that the more positive disposition manifested overall by the girls appeared to be particularly accentuated in mixed arrangements.

Morris (Morris, 1978) examined the attitudes to French at the transfer point between middle school (9-13 years) and high school (13-18 years) of 374 pupils in the north of England. Whereas boys' attitudes were never very positive and declined after transfer, he also found that the more favourable attitudes of girls also declined as their ethnocentricity increased with age. In other words, they became far more interested in their own identity and culture as they moved into the senior school.

Buckby (Buckby, 1981), also working in the north of England, turned his attention to lesson content, methodology and assessment procedures. In particular, he was commissioned to study the effects of the implementation of teaching French by graded objectives. One of the principal successes of this innovation, he claimed, was the manifestation of more positive attitudes in teachers and learners, and notably the narrowing of the traditional gap between boys' and girls' attitude scores.

Eardley (Eardley, 1984) surveyed the opinions of 388 sixth form students in Wales in an attempt to identify the main reasons for the failure of languages to attract recruits to Advanced level courses. For many stated reasons there were noticeable sex differences, but no tests of statistical significance were applied. Of course, in many cases, the results of studies at this level are governed by, and confirm, decisions made much earlier in a pupil's schooling, usually before or at the option stage.

HMI (HMI, 1985a) were able to interview 560 fourth year boys in their survey of schools with a relatively high uptake in languages. They talked to those who had chosen to continue with a modern language, those who had opted out and those who were obliged to take a language in the fourth year. Apparently, certain features of foreign language learning were regularly singled out as enjoyable by the boys irrespective of whether they were continuing with a language or not. Least popular activities cited were written work, grammar, learning verbs and uninteresting books. Among those who had opted in, the principal reasons cited are given below:

Table 15:   Reasons for continuing with a modern language

Enjoyment	109
Modern language useful in career	88
Success in the first 3 years	80
Most interesting subject in option pool	46
Wish to communicate	24
Other reasons	25
	372

(n = 225 - Pupils often gave more than one reason)

SOURCE: HMI, 1985a

These 'findings' tend to confirm the notion that early success in learning a language is likely to lead to a more positive desire to continue with the subject. It highlights the importance also of 'selling' languages as relevant to careers. Most of all, however, it illustrates how pupils (in this case boys, but the same must be true for girls too) respond positively to stimulating teaching and enjoyable lesson content. In other words, the affective dimension is the key to improving the uptake of pupils for language courses. It is, after all, human nature to wish to prolong pleasurable experiences.

What the boys in the HMI survey enjoyed most of all was oral work in the foreign language. A few years ago, I was inclined to believe that boys were more likely to shun this activity. I wrote:

'One result of the introduction of largely oral-based methods could be that the emphasis on repetition, question and answer sequences and pattern practice has discouraged rather than motivated pupils. While girls may conform more readily to teacher requests for responses, boys object more strongly than girls to being asked to involve themselves in what they may see as meaningless chatter.' (Powell & Littlewood, 1982)

In the light of the evidence more recently accrued should I now amend this view? Or had the teachers in the survey schools found a new, more exhilarating formula for oral exploitation of language? Even the boys in the HMI survey schools who had opted out of languages for a number of reasons ranked oral work as the most enjoyable aspect of foreign language lessons.

In a detailed case-study of one Nottinghamshire mixed comprehensive school, O'Brien (O'Brien, 1985) also found that 'speaking French' did not appear to be less popular with boys than with girls. He does, however, qualify this by adding:

'Whereas speaking French in front of a large class audience may

48

be an ordeal, to a small group of one's peers it may be an enjoyable activity.' (p62)

In a much larger survey of pupil attitudes involving 953 second year
pupils in 6 mixed comprehensive schools in the south west of England
(part of the University of Bath project) the attitude scale admin-
istered encompassed five sub-categories, namely: importance of the
foreign language, ethnocentricity, self-image, attitudes towards
writing and attitudes towards oral work. Girls, in line with pre-
vious pilot studies, scored higher overall, but the least difference
in scores occurred in those aspects reflecting attitudes to oral
work, where the positive attitudes expressed by girls across the
schools were shared by most of the boys in the sample. In one school
boys actually had a marginally better opinion of oral work than
girls. These same boys, it turned out, presented an interesting set
of results in other aspects of the attitude scale. For example,
their scores for each of the categories 'importance', 'self-image'
and 'writing' were higher than those of the girls in the same year
group. Unfortunately, it is impossible to ascertain why precisely.
So many factors will have influenced their opinions about learning
French as they progressed through their first year. One thing, however, is certain. That particular language department has high
expectations of its pupils, a well-defined programme of work and
examination results which are consistently very good.

Eighteen months later the same cohort of pupils were surveyed for a
second time. An important question in the minds of the researchers
was whether the enthusiasm for oral work expressed at the beginning
of the second year would extend into the final weeks of the third
year. When the results were collated, it was found that the difference in attitude scores for oral items between boys and girls had,
in fact, diminished considerably. In the second year the gap between
mean scores had been 0.4 (significant at $p = 0.01$). The discrepancy
at the end of the third year was extremely slight however (0.028)
and certainly no longer statistically significant.

The opportunity to speak the foreign language in the course of
learning may be a redeeming feature for pupils. In general, it must
be said that enquiries into the relative popularity of languages
among those subjects offered in school are yielding less encouraging
results for the language teacher. The survey mentioned above (Powell
and Batters, 1985) also included questions relating to subject preferences. The extent to which a foreign language is a comparatively
unpopular subject, even after only one year's study, soon became
apparent, for a language was cited as being least favourite subject
for 141 pupils (14.8%). In all, 37.4% expressed some degree of dislike of a language. As expected, girls were more likely to express a
preference for a language than boys.

Table 16:   Unpopularity of a foreign language

	Girls	%	Boys	%	All pupils	%
Least favourite subject	53	10.7	88	19.2	141	14.7
Strong dislike	51	10.3	60	13.1	111	11.6
Dislike	62	12.5	44	9.5	106	11.1
Total dislikes	166	33.5	192	41.8	358	37.4

(n = 953: 494 girls; 459 boys)

Table 17:   Popularity of a foreign language

	Girls	%	Boys	%	All pupils	%
Favourite subject	24	4.8	7	1.5	31	3.2
Next favourite	64	12.9	36	7.8	100	10.5
Like subject	63	12.7	50	10.9	113	11.8
Total likes	151	30.4	93	20.2	244	25.5

(n = 953: 494 girls; 459 boys)

We have to accept that the idea of mastering a foreign language is alien - if that is not too strong a word - to many British people, and apathy and possibly apprehension are all too easily transmitted from generation to generation. And yet, schools can make a difference. The learning experience itself and the values trasmitted by the school can play a vital part in re-educating young minds to a more equitable approach by presenting an alternative frame of reference.

We need now, therefore, to scrutinise more fully the complex network of factors within school that influence children's perceptions.

I am assuming that all language teachers would wish to increase the numbers of boys and girls pursuing successfully a sustained course of foreign language study. So, what is happening inside schools and inside foreign language classrooms that might contribute to the growing imbalance between the sexes? What can schools, language departments and individual teachers do to redress the balance? These are the crucial questions which will occupy us in the next chapter.

4

Gender differences in school and the drop-out problem: causes and remedies

The value placed upon learning a foreign language by pupils is, undoubtedly, enormously influenced by public attitudes to the countries where the language is spoken. A foreign language, usually French, may ostensibly be the only really 'new' subject in the curriculum of eleven or twelve-year-olds as they enter secondary schools. However, they will already have formed opinions about the speakers of the language and, by association, about the merits of learning more about them through the lessons to come.

We are, geographically and psychologically, an insular nation. It does not take long for the media in the United Kingdom, especially some elements of the popular press, to stir up nationalistic fervour which can so easily overflow into jingoism. Then people who inhabit other parts of the globe are seen as inferior and their customs and practices as bizarre, if not downright ridiculous.

Research findings suggest that boys tend to be more ethnocentric than girls; they are less interested in other cultures, supposedly more self-sufficient in their own group identity. How can language teachers promote their subjects and, at the same time, combat some of the insidious prejudices that are formed in pupils' minds outside school?

There are reasons for believing that boys are less kindly disposed to the new experience of foreign-language learning than girls and likely to remain so as long as they study a language but, generally speaking, all first-year pupils are keen and motivated to learn. How can schools nurture and sustain this initial enthusiasm? How can pupils be convinced of the intrinsic and instrumental worth of acquiring a foreign language?

Raising the status of language learning in the minds of pupils and the general public is the task that now faces the language teaching profession. It will not be easy. What strategies can be adopted in the classroom and in the community of the school to improve the image of foreign languages, and thereby improve take-up rates?

These are some of the questions that will be tackled in this chapter. Under various headings I shall review a range of factors that I believe influence boys' and girls' opinions of languages. It is the pupils' perspective which is uppermost in my mind. Following each section I shall list a series of suggestions under the label

Remedies. My dictionary provides several definitions for this word, one of which is 'a means of removing or counteracting or relieving any evil'. I doubt whether many people would define the sex imbalance in languages as an evil! Yet, at the risk of uttering hyperbole, I personally consider it a sin that so much talent is currently being wasted among our pupils. Competence in one or more foreign languages is the normal expectation of many other nations' children, female and male. There are many of our minority communities' children who already exhibit bilingual or trilingual skills. Ability to speak a foreign language should be deemed an asset by State and society. In Britain, however, monoglottism is an endemic disease which afflicts the vast majority of its citizens. It is time some remedies were proposed and prescribed.

Some of the recommendations made will be beyond the scope of the individual teacher or department, but most are not. There is some repetition as various points are made. This, maybe, is necessary to reinforce the central messages of the chapter. It will obviously help if the whole school staff is involved in formulating policy for equal opportunities and, naturally, if that policy is implemented energetically by all people within the establishment. Some schools already have appointed an equal opportunities coordinator with the intention of monitoring practice and initiating programmes of staff development leading to greater awareness of inequalities within the system. These have hitherto been directed in most cases to curriculum areas such as science, technology and craft but language departments cannot afford not to be involved. Stereotyping by sex disadvantages both women and men in our society and affects the whole of school practices. Schools bear a major responsibility for perpetuating stereotypes of all forms, but schools can also be significant agents of change.

Factor 1: Status and provision

i) Matriculation

Foreign languages have enjoyed relatively high subject status in the school curriculum for most of this century. This is not unconnected with the view of language learning as a discipline, a trainer of the mind, a developer of analytical and logical skills, hence generally reserved only for the brightest. It has even been doubted whether the female brain could cope with the strain!

> 'It is certainly rare to find girls whose minds the study of French seems to have done anything to strengthen or train'
> (Schools Enquiry Commission Report, 1868, vol 9,
> cited in Partington and Luker, 1984, p69).

Ability to master a foreign language, at least in terms of the translation skills required to pass exams, was adjudged a good pre-

52

dictor of high academic achievement so it became a matriculation requirement for university entrance in virtually all specialisms. Regrettably, since the sixties fewer and fewer universities make such demands on their future undergraduates. Only one or two of the older establishments hold out with requests for an '0' level pass in a foreign language. The status of languages in school took a tumble when this easing of entry requirements began, and it has continued to decline ever since. Subsequently foreign languages seldom feature in the core curriculum 11-16 at least in state maintained schools.

ii) Examinations post-16

There is currently little opportunity for pupils staying on in the sixth form to pursue non-specialist language courses. The usual 'A' level package does not allow a great deal of curriculum time for innovations at this level, but some schools have begun to experiment with courses which offer students recognised qualifications outside the usual exam boards (Institute of Linguists, London Chamber of Commerce, etc.). 'AS' levels go some way towards opening opportunities for non-specialist linguists to continue with a language beyond the age of 16, provided, that is, they have stayed the course until '0' level.   There really ought to be room as well for ab initio language courses. There are plenty of teachers qualified to teach languages other than French and German who would welcome the chance to work with their 'other' languages.

iii) Options

Reduction to option status has had dire consequences for languages. The way subjects are organised into option blocks is crucial. There are still schools where pupils are offered a 'straight' choice between physics and French. This obviously creates a sex-stereotypical polarisation of choices. How much longer will French groups remain viable there? In other schools, pupils have difficult decisions to take regarding a third science or a second language and the pressure to present a full battery of science subjects is mounting year by year. Elsewhere a language has to compete with history or geography, or there appears to pupils to be a definite division between academic and practical subjects when the first foreign language is in the option block alongside technical drawing, metalwork, domestic science or needlework. This arrangement is not only likely to perpetuate an elitist view of languages, it is also likely to reinforce sex-stereotyping.

iv) Counselling

The way option schemes are devised and presented is central to our concerns. A study of the literature that parents and pupils receive can be very revealing. I recently read one booklet which included the phrase 'And girls considering office work are well advised to keep up a foreign language' (sic). Leaving aside the glaringly sexist nature of this advice, there was simply no mention of boys with regard to languages. Careers teachers and the local careers advisory service need to be fully conversant with job opportunities involving languages. In the increasingly competitive world of education, language teachers themselves need to sell their subjects to all concerned.

v) Publicity

The status of a subject can be measured overtly by factors such as pupil numbers, time allocation, the number of staff with posts of responsibility, examination results, etc, but there are numerous covert factors operating too which determine how pupils, parents and other teachers rank a specialist subject department. In one local school I visit regularly the languages department makes its presence felt all over the building by displays of pupils' work, exhibitions, posters, foreign labels and realia. Walls, ceiling and stairways are covered. Even the instructions for using the staff telephone are in French! Another department has produced a brochure advertising its linguistic talents and offering services of translating, interpreting, letter-writing and travel advice to pupils, parents and colleagues. Some may consider this a debasement of their appointed function but it has, in the jargon, put this department 'on the map' locally. A year ago I was invited to participate in 'une semaine française' at a school. This involved literally everyone. A special programme of teaching was worked out involving as many references to France and things French as possible, across the curriculum. The school took on the aspect of a French collège with everyone from Directeur to Concièrge involved in creating an authentic atmosphere with direction signs, name plates, labels, flags, displays, etc. Dinner staff concocted French delicacies which were chalked up on the daily menu board in that language. Lunchtime activities included 'concours de boules', discothèques with French pop music and French computer programs. The tuck shop refused to sell goods to anyone not in possession of French franc tokens obtained from an adjacent bureau de change. Increased interest in and motivation to learn languages may not be guaranteed by the organisation of this type of event, but it is worth a try.

vi) French and other languages

Like many people, I believe that the dominance of French is an undesirable feature of current provision. The claims from interested parties that other languages should be given greater priority can be justified on several grounds, not least variety of choice. The second language is usually offered only on a restricted basis to those who have a good track record in the first foreign language. These pupils then take on the immensely difficult (not to say unrealistic) task of presenting themselves for public examination

54

after considerably less exposure to the subject than any other in the curriculum.

Stopping short of making German or Spanish the first foreign language taught, some schools now raise two languages to first foreign language status, either by alternating the language on a yearly basis or by offering one language to half of one year's intake and the other to the rest.

Two of the schools in the University of Bath project do just that, one by an arbitrary division of the first year intake into two different language groups, the other by offering an element of parental choice of language. In the latter case, numbers have, over the years, been reasonably evenly distributed. One administrative advantage is that newcomers during the school year have a choice of language classes to attend. More important is the fact that pupils are able to make better informed decisions when selecting a language course at the option stage. This pattern of provision <u>can</u> produce viable groups in the fourth year in both languages and both sexes.

There is perhaps some germ of truth in the widely held view that boys respond more positively to German than French, but under normal arrangements only a minority of boys are likely to be presented with the chance of learning German since, by the time this second language is introduced to the 'ablest' linguists, most of the boys will have lost their way and lost their place in the top sets.

We should not forget that Britain is really a multilingual society now, because of the presence here of settled communities who regularly use a language other than English in their daily lives. A number of schools with a multilingual intake support the teaching of these community languages on an informal basis, that is, outside the usual timetable, but ideally this teaching should become more widely available. It should take place within the normal curriculum, and should not be restricted to those who have these languages as their mother tongue. Table 18 (see p56) gives some idea of the number of examination entries involved a few years ago.

There are important messages emerging from studying these figures. The sex imbalance in candidature, where it exists, is the reverse of the other, traditionally taught modern languages. It should however also be noted that speakers of the minority community languages often experience school timetabling difficulties if they wish to study, and be examined in, both a community language and a traditionally taught modern language. Language skills, not just in the mother tongue, are prized by speakers of our community languages, both female and male. It is a shame that the majority of the British population do not share these values.

Table 18:   'O' and 'A' level entries in minority languages: 1981

| | O Level | | | A Level | | |
	Males	Females	Total	Males	Females	Total
ENTRIES						
Afrikaans	98	66	164	-	-	-
Arabic (modern)	59	27	86	-	1	1
Chinese (modern)	904	534	1,438	161	80	241
Dutch	80	77	157	20	28	48
Greek (modern)	249	367	616	117	114	231
Gujarati	75	96	171	-	-	-
Hebrew (modern)	98	99	197	13	22	35
Hindi	60	75	135	17	12	29
Irish	163	23	186	-	-	-
Malay	175	126	301	-	-	-
Persian (modern)	165	84	269	1	2	3
Polish	169	233	402	64	93	157
Portuguese	95	107	202	17	16	33
Punjabi	77	125	202	6	5	11
Turkish	96	80	176	25	25	50
Urdu	181	124	305	65	26	91
Others (excl. Welsh)	252	236	488	60	74	134
TOTAL	2,996	2,479	5,475	566	498	1,064

Source: Examination Boards, England and Wales

vii) Setting by sex

Experiments in single-sex setting for science and maths within the mixed school have in recent years been a source of some controversy. Originally, the idea was introduced as a way of improving the performance of girls. It was assumed that by taking them out of classes where boys dominated numerically and vocally, girls would gain a better self-image, receive better attention from the teacher and be free to explore concepts unfamiliar to them in their own way and in their own time. In one school where this occurred the girls' achievement did seem to improve quite dramatically in science and maths (Smith, 1984). The results of the Girls into Science and Technology (GIST) project, however, were equivocal (Whyte, 1985).

In languages, such experiments are rare. In one school involved in the University of Bath project, where some sixty pupils were segregated by sex for French from the beginning of the second to the end of the third year teacher opinions were split as to the success or otherwise of the experiment. One thing, however, is certain: the take-up rate for languages is exceptionally high in this school. There is only as small margin of difference between the sexes. With both French and German offered as first foreign language in the first years, pupils can pick up the second language in the second year. The take-up for French was 71.3% for girls and 68.7% for boys; for German the figures were 45.3% girls and 45.8% boys.

It is difficult to draw many firm conclusions from these outcomes. The take-up rate, for example, could easily have been more strongly affected by other factors, e.g. teacher quality or the aptitude and preferences of that particular year group, not to mention the design of the option scheme. Until more schools opt to try out such experiments and the process and results can be rigorously evaluated, the effects of teaching languages in single-sex groupings are still debatable. Nevertheless, notable positive aspects of this kind of arrangement are that more boys and girls are guaranteed access to 'top set teaching', teachers' expectations are raised, and programmes of work devised can take particular notice of sex-specific interests should these arise.

Status and provision - proposed remedies

* The Committee of Vice-Chancellors and Principals (CVCP) should reconsider matriculation requirements for entrance to undergraduate courses. A pass at 'O' level in a foreign language should normally be required for all degree courses.

* The new system of 'AS' levels should be promoted in schools especially for the benefit of non-specialist linguists.

* Opportunities for learning foreign languages ab initio should be introduced in the 16-19 age range.

* Schools should endeavour to introduce more practical foreign language courses leading to alternative exam qualifications such as those of the Institute of Linguists (IL) and the London Chamber of Commerce and Industry (LCCI). The Foreign Languages at Work scheme (FLAW) is a particularly welcome initiative.

* The inclusion of a foreign language in the common curriculum should be viewed as a high priority. This would not only 'obviate the possible creation of a hierarchy of subjects in option schemes' (HMI, 1985a, p21) but would bring this country into line with our partners in Europe.

* Where option schemes exist they should be constructed in such a way as to avoid the creation of likely sex-polarisation through the juxtaposition of science and a language.

* As a step towards including a foreign language in the common curriculum, it is necessary 'to provide curricular arrangements which encourage the majority of pupils (and therefore many more boys) to continue the study of a modern language at the option stage' (HMI, 1985a, p21).

* The full implications of option choices need to be spelt out in detail and repeated over a period of time to parents and pupils. Counselling and guidance prior to choice and associated documentation must be free of sex-stereotypical expectations. Pupils should be supported if they elect to take non-traditional courses.

* Language teachers should monitor carefully the way their subjects are presented to pupils by the school. Departments should promote languages by means of posters, displays, outside speakers, films, tape-slide sequences, videotapes, etc. Work opportunities involving languages should be highlighted in order to dissuade boys and girls from abandoning languages.

* Language departments should consider ways in which they can publicise their presence in the school and community. Boys and girls together should prepare events for language days, evenings or weeks. Such co-operative ventures should not be seen as impinging on the normal programme of work, rather as being an integral part of purposeful language learning. Festivals of Languages involving many different schools can act as a real boost for pupils in the participating schools.

* Schools should experiment with different patterns of provision. If staffing and pupil numbers permit, two languages should be offered with equal first foreign language status.

* Single-sex setting does not automatically improve the learning

experience of either sex, but as a short-term measure it may alleviate some of the difficulties boys may experience in mixed groups and thus improve take-up rates.

Factor 2: Teachers and teaching

i) Staffing

It is bound to seem undesirable to some readers to take into account the sex of a teacher as a possible factor in the sex imbalance in languages among pupils. Accusations of sexism trip off the tongue very easily. Besides, according to the official figures studied in Chapter 2, the actual sex imbalance among language staff is much less pronounced than is popularly believed. So why persist? In conversations with teachers and in written answers to questions on the language drop-out problem in general, 'sex of teacher' is regularly presented as a probable contributory factor. Some comments have been quite blunt: 'There is a surfeit of female language teachers' (woman). Others have made what may be an oversimplistic causal link: 'Four out of five members of staff are female here thus perpetuating the idea it is a girls' subject' (man). If these responses are typical of teachers' opinions across the country - and they are merely examples from a large stock - the issue of a teacher's sex does seem to warrant further scrutiny. In doing this, it is vital to attempt to gauge pupils' perceptions of gender, because what teachers believe pupils think and what the pupils really feel may not be wholly identical.

Results of research in the past few years suggest that the sex of a language teacher is irrelevant, as indeed it should be. In the University of Bath project, over 900 pupils in the six case study schools, all mixed comprehensives, were asked two questions about their teachers. The first was purely factual, relating to their experience of female or male staff.

Table 19:   3rd year pupils' experience of female and male teachers

	Taught only by a man		Taught only by a woman		Taught by both men and women	
Girls	27	5.5%	114	29.8%	312	64.5% n=483
Boys	20	4.5%	99	22.2%	325	73.2% n=444
All pupils	47	5.0%	243	26.2%	637	68.7% n=927

In the language departments of these schools the ratio of female to male staff was 1.25:1. The fact that nearly 70% of pupils in the schools had been taught by both men and women may have presented them with a more neutral view of adult involvement in the language teaching world than pupils in many other schools.

The second question invited pupils to state preferences. Table 20 summarises the results.

Table 20:   Pupil preference for female or male teachers

	Prefer a man		Prefer a woman		No preference	
Girls	17	3.5%	69	14.2%	397	82.1% n=483
Boys	39	8.7%	61	13.7%	344	77.4% n=444
All pupils	56	6.0%	130	14.0%	741	79.9% n=929

The overwhelming rejection among 14-year-olds of any idea that one sex of teacher is to be preferred to the other is an important result of this research. Maybe similar research should now be pursued in schools where there are many more female teachers of languages than men; but I doubt, myself, whether the reactions of the pupils would be significantly different. Nevertheless, it seems advisable that, whenever circumstances permit, pupils gain experience of being taught by both female and male staff during their first three years of learning a language.

Systematic observation of these same pupils in the project schools over one calendar year spanning second and third year classes also provided some interesting revelations. Of course, an observer cannot be omnipresent, watching everything going on during lesson time, so any accumulation of data risks producing an oversimplistic view of the different forms of interaction taking place in the language classroom and the activities pupils are engaged in. On first analysis it appeared that pupils observed in classes taught by women spent a greater portion of their time than those in male-taught classes on observing, listening to the tape, the teacher and other pupils, talking in the foreign language, writing, doing group-work exercises and 'showing spontaneity'. In contrast, pupils in classes taught by male teachers spent more time on reading, talking to other pupils, using the mother tongue and being less involved. But the differences are slight and indeed, as expected, differences between teachers of the same sex were more in evidence. Overall the results tended to suggest that the activities occuring in a foreign language class are not affected in any marked way by the sex of the teacher.

ii) Teaching approaches

(a) Didactics

Language learning is a cumulative process. Although contemporary teaching approaches may minimise the linear nature of language acquisition, it soon becomes apparent to pupils that knowledge gained (or lost) during the early stages is vital for success at all later stages. Many school subjects emphasise the overall experience of learning and possibly teachers place more value on the awareness derived from the process than the retention of factual knowledge. In other subjects, discovery learning and individualised instruction are normal. With languages, however, it is the developing competence that is rewarded; competence that has to be demonstrated by (accurate?) production of spoken and written language; it cannot be taken for granted. Whole class teaching and didactic methods prevail and persist (Westgate, 1985).

Mastery of a language under school conditions depends heavily on the possession or the development of a good short-term and long-term memory. It is surely in the foreign language lesson that the pupil is called upon most frequently to practise through repetition, memorise and recall – and it is in the language classroom where errors, incompetence and forgetfulness are most in evidence. Making mistakes is part of the process of language learning, but it is difficult for learners to comprehend this unique feature even if teachers take the trouble to explain why. It is even harder for them to appreciate it if they are being corrected after every utterance. Nobody likes to be told he or she is wrong. Furthermore, in many schools pupils are convinced from very early on that 'work' is synonymous with 'writing'. Consequently oral activities, especially if they are presented as games, may be fun – but they are seen as momentary diversions, not really associated with 'work', and so devalued. Talk is, of course, an essential ingredient of foreign language lesson time, but talk must be productive; that is, it must be developed with communicative goals in view.

If the above is a fair representation of life in schools, the consequences for the boy-girl imbalance may be more than hypothetical. By the time boys reach secondary school they have been conditioned to consider that 'manipulating', 'constructing' and 'doing' things are forms of behaviour – and this includes learning behaviour – expected of and appropriate for them. The 'Girls into Science' lobby recognises this and urges schools to take every opportunity, for example:

> 'to provide girls with extra experience in using tools and unfamiliar equipment ... to help care for apparatus, assist in

putting it out, collecting and checking it and even carrying out simple repairs.' (Harding, 1983, p38)

It is hoped that by deliberate policies such as these, girls' self-image in relation to science may be enhanced.

What of boys' self-esteem in relation to languages? No child relishes the thought of spending hours just listening, repeating and being called upon to answer questions to which no one really needs to know the answer or to which the answer is already known. But girls hitherto (but for how much longer?) have been conditioned into complying more readily with teachers' wishes and may accept such processes as a necessary means to an end.

(b) The products of language learning

The trouble seems to be that there is often no visible, no tangible result for all that frenetic activity - frenetic at least for the teacher. To use Eric Hawkins' (Hawkins, 1981) terms, 'rehearsal' without 'performance' eventually becomes meaningless. Boys and girls would benefit from a style of language learning in which the language acquired is applied as soon as possible in some constructive way. Within the classroom this will mean designing posters, charts, diagrams, writing letters that will be posted, setting out displays of drawn or written work, even making mobiles which will dangle from the ceiling! It will also involve pupils in performing sketches, carrying out surveys, making recordings such as compiling and producing a radio programme, or using video. Units of work should, whenever possible, be presented in some form to an 'audience' different from the peer group: pupils in the foreign country linked by exchanges of photos, letters, comics, cassettes, parcels containing all sorts of items. Failing this, or in addition, the audience can be pupils in another local school, other classes within the year group, pupils lower down the school, other teachers, parents, governors, and on more ambitious occasions the local press and radio.

Boys might also benefit at the present time if language learning presented them with greater scope for problem solving. Working with microcomputers is an obvious example, provided that the programs offer a real challenge and are not merely automated vocabulary or grammar tests. International links via school computer networks will offer a marvellous opportunity for direct, immediate access to teachers and pupils in the target language country. Microcomputer enthusiasts can also, of course, design their own programs for language learning and testing which may provide increased motivation to study the language itself. A word of caution is necessary, however. There are already signs that computer technology is becoming yet another all-male preserve. While micros may provide a useful intrinsic incentive to boys, teachers should ensure that girls receive their fair share as far as access to machines, advice and encouragement are concerned. Other simulations and role-plays in which there is a genuine information gap can provide stimulating experience for pairs or small groups even at an early phase in language learning. This presupposes greater use of the foreign language by teacher and pupils and striving to create realistic contexts in which to practise and extend language usage.

(c) The teacher's role

The role of the language teacher is changing. Communicative methodology makes greater demands on a teacher's inventiveness and ability to establish good relationships with pupils. It demands a less imposing presence, a less autocratic stance and a greater tolerance of error. Reticent pupils - who may, of course, be boys or girls - need constant encouragement to participate, without fear of censure or ridicule from teacher or peer-group for uttering or writing inaccurate phrases. Pupils should not feel they are walking a tightrope of failure every time they speak or commit words to paper. Being made to perform in the public arena of the classroom can be daunting for some boys and girls. Extrovert pupils - more often boys than girls (?) - need to be challenged into producing more than mindless repetition or single-word responses to closed questions.

Teachers must not fall into the trap of expecting boys to have more difficulties than girls with language learning activities such as pronunciation or written work. Work should be presented with no differing expectations of involvement or achievement between boys and girls. Similarly, to create artificial competition between the sexes, for example in team games or group activities, is wholly undesirable.

In sets consisting predominantly of girls (so often the top-ability sets and exam classes) teachers should be sensitive to the needs of the boys who form the minority. These boys may be subjected to incredible pressure from their male peers to abandon languages or underperform. They must be supported in their 'untraditional' choice of course of study.

There can be a tendency among inexperienced teachers to respond mostly to pupils who display their willingness to participate in the lesson by raising hands or eagerly proffering answers. Interaction research in mixed science classes shows that a teacher's time is seldom distributed equitably between the sexes (Whyte, 1984). Male domination and attention-seeking is rife! This phenomenon seems also to be manifested in foreign language lessons, so teachers really need to be conscious of the risks of sex bias in their attention giving. There are considerable difficulties for teachers in deciding how much time to devote to individual pupils or groups of pupils within their classes, but awareness of the dangers of an uneven allocation of time can help.

It needs to be more widely recognised that the present low involvement of boys in foreign languages is unacceptable; that it is inex-
pedient, if not inadmissable, that so many pupils give up so readily
at the age of 14. There is no substitute for good teaching. If a
language department builds up a reputation for itself by producing
rewarding, interesting lessons, presenting exciting projects and
initiatives and maintaining a good record of examination successes,
it is likely to attract many more boys and girls to courses in the
fourth and fifth years and into the sixth form.

iii) Teaching materials and subject matter

    'She wants to become a doctor like her father.
    He wants to become an engineer like his mother.'
    (Russian textbook for teaching English)

It is highly improbable that such statements could be found in
foreign-language teaching texts in use in Britain. The writer of
these sentences, of course, could be accused of misrepresenting
normal British patterns of employment by providing a woman engineer
as a model to be emulated because, as we know only too well, there
are currently very few women pursuing careers in engineering in this
country. Foreign-language textbooks, as indeed textbooks for most
school subjects, remain conservative in that the images they present
of different societies and cultures are those based on conventional,
frequently outmoded stereotypes of female and male roles and status.
As such they are sexist and treat women unjustly.

The extent to which foreign language textbooks in common use dis-
criminate against women has been well documented by several writers.
Gaff (Gaff, 1982), for example, pointed accusing fingers at a couple
of popular French courses. He highlighted the way in which stereotypical images can be found not just in the distribution of res-
ponsibilities within the family, but in the range and variety of
activities which male characters enjoy but which are denied to
female characters. Examples were cited from various elements of the
course books: illustrations, reading matter, dialogues and even
grammatical exercises.

Earlier, two more writers (Hartman and Judd, 1978), reviewing texts
for teaching English as a second language in the United States,
pointed out the risks of omission and one-sided role-allocation.
More recently a team of language teachers working in London produced
a set of Guidelines for teachers of languages (ILEA, 1984). These
anti-sexist guidelines - the term 'anti-' clearly indicative of an
interventionist policy - review options and vocational guidance. But
the bulk of their report concentrates on an analysis of texts and,
most usefully, on providing a detailed set of suggestions to
teachers for avoiding reinforcing sex-stereotypes. They show ways of

presenting an alternative view of the world even by some minor adjustments to illustrations or text. They include in their <u>Guidelines</u> the checklist used for their programme of textual analysis.

Of course, as these enterprising teachers acknowledge:

> 'It is quite unrealistic to expect that by only making some changes in the language lesson the problem of sex differentiation will be overcome.' (ILEA, 1984, p1-2)

Personally, I am doubtful that the sex-stereotyping which permeates many language-teaching textbooks contributes directly to boys' or girls' disenchantment with language study. I suspect that in terms of the lessons they attend there are other features of subject matter that fail to appeal to adolescent tastes. Nonetheless, language departments cannot divest themselves of their responsibility when it comes to combatting sexism within our education system. Besides, it is evident that they have much to gain from any measure that reduces sexist imagery in subject content.

The irrelevance and inappropriateness of the language and situations used to assess pupils in public examinations at 16+ has been demonstrated with vigour by Moys et al (Moys, 1980). Many children may find the courses leading to these examinations less than fully stimulating. At a time when pupils in the third year may be building their own electric motors in physics, designing complex graphics in the computer room and coming to terms with concepts such as hierarchies of settlement and population distribution in geography – what are they up to in French lessons? Could it be that the preponderance of anodyne topics such as shopping, the home, food, clothes, animals, weather, etc acts as a disincentive to boys and girls who might wish to spend their time on more robust topics and provocative areas of interest? In recent years, several publishers have, thankfully, abandoned the artificiality of providing as focus and storyline a make-believe family living in a make-believe, supposedly foreign scenario. The format of new textbooks has improved dramatically with greater flexibility and variety built in for teacher and learner. There is still some way to go, however, before the mismatch between pupils' level of sophistication in the modern world and the childishness of some of the topics and activities presented is overcome completely.

It is essential that language departments review regularly the materials they use. In times of financial cutbacks it is difficult to update resources which contain glaringly out of date, sexist images. The multicultural dimension should not be overlooked wherever the school is situated. Very few textbooks take full account of multiracial, multicultural and multilingual Britain. It is too glib to ask teachers to produce their own materials, although some departments have concentrated their energies and capitation on designing carefully written worksheets or workbooks which more accurately reflect pupils' interests and contemporary life. Not all schools are furnished with good quality reprographic facilities, however, so a departmental policy should be agreed regarding the strategies to be employed with texts. Overtly sexist or racist language or situations should be avoided or at the very least challenged by teachers with their classes. Alternatives to the male-dominated, all-white world can be found.

In order to ascertain what the consumers' preferences are, language teachers should occasionally survey their classes, inviting comments about language learning activities or topics they would like to cover on the course. According to one teacher trainer who has done this regularly, pupils complete questionnaires about lesson contents in a helpful and responsible way, especially when they realise that future lessons will be considerably influenced by their replies. A description of the process and results together with a copy of the questionnaire used can be found in Buckby (Buckby, 1979). With some classes it might be appropriate to use the survey as an opportunity for language work by detailing the preferences, likes and dislikes of the group on wallcharts, writing reports or presenting oral reports of the information accrued from one group to another — in the foreign language, of course.

Studying and plotting the pupil responses in this kind of survey will enable teachers to be better placed to include in their lessons activities which will appeal more directly to their pupils. After all, it is a commonsense view of learning theory that states that the more control a learner has over the material to be learnt, the greater the motivation to learn.

iv) <u>Assessment</u>

As part of my continuing enquiries into various features of the sex imbalance in foreign language learning in Britain, I have, naturally, on many occasions sought the advice and opinions of practising teachers. On one occasion teachers from 42 mixed comprehensive schools provided me with numerous comments in a free response section of a questionnaire. Views were expressed on pupils' biological and social development, their classroom behaviour, their differing reactions to lessons, their expressed ideas about the foreigners whose language they were studying — and so on. There were also some poignant remarks about parental influence or lack of it, social values and career considerations. Materials, option systems and staffing were also duly reviewed. However, having sorted out the comments into categories under labels such as these, I discovered that the highest pile of cards occurred under the heading Assessment. I reproduce, verbatim, a number of these teachers' statements below. The reasons for my selection and the sequence should become obvious.

'Boys tend to perform much worse in written exercises from their arrival from primary school (our assessments are mainly based on written work).'

'Boys seem to master the oral/aural side more easily than writing. This causes frustration when emphasis is placed on written accuracy too soon.'

'Insistence on accuracy and neatness in years 1 and 2 by teachers - girls achieve this better.'

'In the early years girls tend to be neater and tidier in presentation which may influence some teachers in their assessment.'

'Teachers over-encourage those who perform better, especially (sometimes) women teachers with bright girls?'

'Credit is given mainly for formal written skills and there is little scope for inventive oral work.'

'In this school there is a tendency for boys to appear 'naughtier' in the first year, thereby inclining teachers to assume they are less able than may actually be the case.'

'I feel we are too easily impressed by the neatness and presentation of girls' work unless made aware of this.'

'If we are to be honest I feel we as teachers are in part responsible for this - it is all too easy to take neat, careful written work produced by girls as evidence of linguistic ability whilst boys, who are probably just as capable, tend not to pay as much attention to this area.'

Already in Chapter 2, I have pointed to the way that the pattern of the sex imbalance in the upper school can be established by what I consider premature setting by ability during or at the end of the first year. Some of these teachers' comments suggest that I may not be alone in my concern.

The second part of this same questionnaire was intended to elicit information about how pupils were assessed prior to setting. Table 21 displays the different tools of assessment in the order of frequency of use.

There is an impressive array of tests being operated in the schools. Clearly, the more complex the assessment procedure, the more time required to administer it, and teachers rightly complain that they are given very little time to make decisions that affect children's lives in a critical way.

Table 21:   Assessment of pupils prior to setting

	Nature of Assessment	No. of tallies
1	Teacher grades awarded on impression of classroom performance	34
2	End of year test (mostly written)	33
3	Coursework (e.g. classroom, homework)	25
4	Formal termly tests	20
5	Graded tests/credit scheme results	6
6	School tests on reception in year 1	4
7=	Aptitude tests	3
7=	other standardised tests	3
9=	Primary school reports	2
9=	VRQ tests	2
9=	Tests in other subjects (e.g. maths)	2
9=	Other processes	2

(n = 42 mixed comprehensive schools)

One school claimed to use a combination of eight different sets of information but the majority used only two. Two schools relied on only one item (no. 6), the teachers in both these schools feeling competent to set pupils by ability well before Christmas in the first year.

The dominance of teacher grades on impression of classroom performance is, perhaps, inevitable. But, as all teachers know, children are adept at creating and reinforcing false impressions of their potential and then performing according to teacher expectations. Besides, it is not always a wise move on a pupil's part to display too much enthusiasm in front of the peer group. Even during the first year, being labelled 'keen' is not seen as a compliment. It is something to be avoided in most pupil sub-cultures. Similarly, gaining high marks for neat, colourful written work, frequently low-level activities such as labelling and drawing, may not always be an indicator of real promise as a linguist.

The graded objectives movement has provided schools involved with further means of assessing pupils on a regular basis. Many of the newer courses on the market include their own package of testing materials providing, in the main, useful information about pupils' oral, aural and reading skills. These should complement more traditional written tests. More extensive use of aptitude tests might also yield better all round information about pupils' potential when used in conjunction with other summative tests.

Much has already been written about the relevance and appropriateness of public examinations at 16+ and 18+. I do not wish to repeat the largely critical arguments put forward. We must accept that knowledge of exam contents filters down through a school and I suspect that foreign language examinations do not get very supportive reactions. Choice is, fortunately, widening at 18+ with innovative exam schemes and syllabuses which emphasise the practical application of language skills. Many language teachers look forward to the GCSE with more optimism than their colleagues in other subjects. But the message of this section is clear. If the assessment procedures used to allocate pupils to ability sets or bands continue to produce such a lop-sided effect and, thereby, deny a fair distribution of places to each of the sexes, then there will continue to be only a minority of able boys who are accessed to courses leading to these important examinations.

Teachers and teaching - proposed remedies

* Every school should create an appointment for an equal opportunities coordinator who should initiate staff development and awareness programmes across the curriculum and monitor school practices.

* Every language department should, in addition, take on responsibility for assessing and regularly reassessing its role within the framework of an equal opportunities philosophy. This would include evaluating the appropriateness of materials, keeping a record of class or set rolls and, through a programme of reciprocal observation or self-appraisal, considering ways in which the actual teaching process might improve for female and male pupils.

* Whenever possible pupils should experience language teaching by both female and male staff during the first three years of secondary school. Team teaching can sometimes present opportunities for pupils to work with teachers of both sexes where one sex is in the minority.

* Any overt or covert suggestion that language teaching is an inappropriate profession for men should be challenged.

* Likewise, boys should be presented, by means of posters, job advertisements, visiting speakers etc, with examples of men successfully pursuing careers where foreign language competence

is an important part of their job. These role models should be drawn from as many different spheres of work as possible.

* Teachers should adopt a less didactic teaching style and aim to provide pupils with more opportunities for individualised learning, pair or group work at all levels.

* There should be more variety in lesson planning – less ritual, more elements of surprise.

* Language work, whenever possible, should yield some tangible, visible product.

* Short-term objectives should be realistic and explained to pupils in accessible terms.

* Teachers should adopt a more flexible attitude towards pupil errors, especially in exploratory oral work.

* Problem-solving activities should be devised which present boys and girls with a worthwhile challenge.

* The foreign language classroom should reflect the foreign culture and provide space for display of pupils' work and that of their contacts abroad.

* The foreign language should, as far as possible, be the medium of instruction as well as the subject matter.

* Teachers should have the highest possible expectations of potential and performance for all their pupils, irrespective of sex.

* A campaign should be launched by every language department to influence those who influence the choices pupils make at the option stage. The wisdom of retaining a foreign language to examination level should be understood by all concerned and transmitted to pupils in the lead-up to option choices.

* Language staff should challenge any written or spoken statement, for example in careers advice, that presents a sex-stereotypical view of society, especially if it impinges on the pupils' perception of the usefulness or relevance of language learning for the different sexes.

* Teaching materials should be reviewed with the purpose of eliminating sexist or racist images or language.

* Each department should possess a coherent scheme of work which takes account of pupil interests and allows some opportunities for exploring conventional female and male topics.

* Parents and colleagues in school should be given a chance to update their impressions of languages in school by attending classes or open evenings where the department's work is explained in detail through observation of lessons, video-recordings, displays of work, equipment, resources etc.

* Language departments in mixed schools should critically review their setting policy. Methods of assessing pupils' abilities and potential should include a battery of tests taking into account all language skills and the differing rates of personal and academic development of the two sexes.

* An annual review of class rolls should be carried out in the mixed school in order to monitor any unwarranted sex imbalance and to investigate causes.

* More research is needed into those processes which affect boys' and girls' readiness to pursue an extended course of foreign language study to examination level at 16+ and 18+.

Factor 3: The pupils themselves

It has been my intention during this review of possible causes for the sex imbalance in languages to keep in mind the pupil perspective of language learning. Yet certain factors still remain unexplored or need reinforcing in this final section.

Languages do not generally feature among the best-loved of school subjects, as has been shown by one of the surveys in the University of Bath project. Summary tables were included in Chapter 3. By the end of the third year, feelings about languages have hardened among these same pupils. Regrettably, even in these six schools which can justifiably be reasonably happy with their language departments' work, especially in their ability to attract a good proportion of pupils staying on beyond the option stage, languages remain among the most unpopular subjects on the time-table.

Table 22: Unpopularity of a foreign language at the end of the third year

	Girls	%	Boys	%	All pupils	%
Least favourite subject	116	24.1	139	31.4	255	27.6
Strong dislike	66	13.7	79	17.8	145	15.7
Dislike	79	16.4	63	14.2	142	15.3
Total dislikes	261	54.2	281	63.4	542	58.6

(n = 925: 482 girls; 443 boys)

Table 23: **Popularity of a foreign language at the end of the third year**

	Girls	%	Boys	%	All pupils	%
Favourite subject	23	4.8	9	2.0	32	3.5
Next favourite	54	11.2	21	4.7	75	8.1
Like subject	69	14.3	38	8.6	107	11.6
Total likes	146	30.3	68	15.5	214	23.2

(n = 925: 482 girls; 443 boys)

With nearly a quarter of the girls and nearly a third of the boys ranking French or German lessons as their least favourite times of the week, these tables do not make joyful reading for anyone. Decidedly there is a lack of intrinsic motivation among young people learning a foreign language, so teachers are forced to develop instrumental incentives to motivate their pupils – and there does not appear to be a superabundance of these. Pupils will stay with a subject if they feel they stand a reasonable chance of succeeding in examinations, but this will apply only to the ablest and even then the examination will often be seen as a means to a different end, i.e. not involving languages. Relevance to one's career is a notion that has to be proved to pupils and currently, in the case of languages, that seems easier to do as far as girls are concerned. It is much more difficult for teachers to influence boys' choices by direct reference to career orientations.

In the meantime, therefore, greater awareness of why pupils are not intrinsically motivated about languages, why they do not enjoy the experience per se, might help to show teachers the way to stimulating greater interest in, and a better response to, the task of acquiring a foreign language. Clearly there are numerous reasons why a school subject should appeal less to some pupils than to others, but children rarely express their dissatisfaction in detailed terms. They prefer to use predictable and unhelpful adjectives such as 'boring'. Occasionally, however, sifting through interview transcripts or questionnaires involving, for the most part, third-year pupils, I come across comments which point to more specific features of lesson content and teaching style.

For some pupils, languages make intolerable demands on their powers of attention and involvement:

'French is very hard, it needs complete concentration' (boy)
'I can't concentrate for that long' (girl)

'I like doing nothing though this is rare with my teacher'
(boy) (!)

Can a foreign language be the only subject in which pupils are expected to <u>learn</u> as opposed to experience? Some pupils seem to think so. This unique claim to exercising the memory is not a point in its favour for some pupils:

'French has too many verbs to learn. It's a good '0' level to have but I would rather get history, geography and biology instead' (girl)

'There's too much to learn which makes it so complicated' (girl)

'I hate learning so many French verbs' (boy)

I have to sympathise with the average third-former who can so easily gain the impression that French has many more tenses than English and ten times as many irregular verbs. German prepositions also appear to present monumental difficulties for most learners. Teachers need to examine very carefully their third-year syllabuses so that some relief is provided from what can so easily become a 'grammar-grind'.

If only more pupils felt like this girl:

'I dislike all the vocab tests but alas! these are important'

or this boy?

'I don't really enjoy French but I would feel defeated if I gave it up'

Such examples of integrative motivation and perseverance are all too infrequent, unfortunately.

Other comments by third-year boys and girls have suggested that foreign language lessons are the source of considerable nervousness and trepidation for some. One or two examples will illustrate possibly why.

'I don't like reading aloud, I feel such a fool' (boy)

'I dislike speaking oral to the teacher (sic) because if you say something wrong you get all embarrassed so the next time you try to get out of doing it' (girl)

'I get upset when teachers get annoyed when you can't pronounce words properly because it's quite difficult to remember every accent, sound and so on' (boy)

'French scares me as it's always so fast moving and leaves me
high and dry' (girl)

The demands on pupil concentration and participation that typify
current approaches to language teaching can certainly act as a
disincentive to continue for some pupils. One local survey directed
at identifying pupils' school-based anxieties produced sobering
results for the French teachers in the county of Somerset. French
was second only to spelling as a focus of pupil fears and worries in
that section dealing with subject-specific aspects.

Table 24:   School anxieties associated with curriculum subjects

Subject	Children ticking this item No.	%
Spelling	323	23
French	295	21
Maths	265	19
Science	157	11
Reading	157	11
PE	132	9.3
English	127	9.0
RE	126	8.9
Games/Sports	119	8.4
Writing	118	8.3
Social Studies	42	3
Art & Crafts	29	2

n = 1406 pupils

SOURCE: Knapman, 1982.

Other reasons for the comparative unpopularity of languages are
probably more associated with instrumental goals, i.e. how useful a
subject appears to further one's career aspirations or educational
advancement. Boys are under a great deal of pressure to do subjects
which adults, especially their parents, consider will be useful to
them. One teacher recently expressed it to me in this way.

'Parents allow girls to opt for subjects they like while boys
have to "prepare for a career"'.

Boys have often decided in the second year whether they are planning
to do a language 'seriously' or not - often they will not. By
emphasising so much the place of science and technology in contemporary society our politicans, the media, our educational planners

and those who fund educational initiatives and research devalue all other curriculum areas, especially, to my mind, languages. It is a sad truth that for young people there does not seem to be any real or pressing need to study languages, other than that of acquiring an extra exam subject.

So what can we do? It would obviously be immoral to create a false impression in the minds of pupils that a qualification in a foreign language will open the door to great wealth and success in any career of their choosing. It is, however, sensible to point out that within the Common Market opportunities for employment may be greater outside Britain and that many barriers to employment have been lifted by EEC legislation. There _are_ highly-paid jobs for professional linguists, but these are available only for the very ablest in possession of postgraduate qualifications in two or more languages. Greater publicity should be given to the fact that a language qualification in conjunction with other specialisms is going to present better chances for employment and career advancement than no language at all. Schools must encourage boys and girls to keep all their options open. To reject languages at 14+ in a shrinking job market is imprudent, to say the least.

At several times during the writing of this Guide, I have warned about the danger of over-simplifications. I have been struck in my discussions with practising teachers how the current unequal representation of boys and girls in foreign language education in this country can be dismissed with remarks such as: 'It has always been like this, I suspect it will stay just the same whatever you do'. This is not only defeatist, it is manifestly not true. Adults assume they understand children's minds all too easily. There is the belief about that boys almost automatically consider languages as 'girls' subjects' and therefore get out at the earliest opportunity. Again, this is a superficial, if not arrogant assumption on the part of those that voice it.

It is appropriate, therefore, to end, as I began, on an optimistic note. I determined early in my own research to ask pupils directly whether they thought it made any difference being a boy or a girl studying a foreign language. If, indeed, they had decided that a pupil's sex does make a difference, I could hardly be accused of putting ideas into their heads. On the contrary, I was pleased to note how overwhelmingly they rejected the ideas

(a) that one sex is more likely to be better at languages than the other

(b) that it is more important for one sex to study languages than the other.

These questions were asked twice, once at the beginning of the

second year and again at the end of the third year. The results look
like this:

Table 25: Pupil perception of relative performance of sexes in
foreign languages

	Boys better %		Girls better %		No difference %	
	2nd yr	3rd yr	2nd yr	3rd yr	2nd yr	3rd yr
Boys	2.2	2.9	4.8	14.7	92.8	82.4
Girls	0.4	1.5	4.4	8.0	95.4	90.5
All pupils	2.6	2.2	9.2	11.2	87.8	86.6

n = 953 in 2nd year, 925 in 3rd year. Missing values 0.4 and 0.0
respectively.

Table 26: Pupil perception of relative importance of foreign
languages for boys and girls

	More important for boys %		More important for girls %		No differnce %	
	2nd yr	3rd yr	2nd yr	3rd yr	2nd yr	3rd yr
Boys	3.3	5.0	1.1	2.7	95.4	92.3
Girls	0.5	0.2	2.2	3.7	97.1	96.1
All pupils	3.8	2.5	3.3	3.2	92.5	94.3

n = 953 in 2nd year, 927 in 3rd year. Missing values 0.4 and 0.0
respectively.

Where pupils did perceive differences, it was generally in support
of their own sex, not unnaturally. The one notable exception is the
shift in some boys' recognition or at least impression that girls
seem to be coping better at languages than themselves. A 10% rise
over two years means that forty or so boys have modified their
opinions. Unfortunately it is impossible to identify exactly which
boys these are, but I suspect that they consist primarily of those
floundering in the bottom sets in the six schools. By and large,
however, it does seem that pupils do resist evaluating their own
performance in languages by direct comparison with their peers of

the opposite sex. Neither do they accord higher value to girls' achievement. In short, given the opportunity to express a view they dismiss some of the sex-stereotypical opinions with which they are credited by teachers, researchers and other adults.

This is good news for those of us who believe it is vital that the drift away from languages by boys and girls should be halted. It also presents us with a challenge. All of us parents, administrators, teacher trainers and student teachers, careers advisers, head-teachers, senior teachers, year tutors, other teachers, other language teachers, need educating about equality of opportunity especially as far as languages are concerned. The value, usefulness, relevance and rewards of foreign language learning need to be publicised – especially to parents for whom the experience of language lessons during their own education some years ago may not have been the most stimulating.

The importance of involving parents is borne out in any investigation into the options process. For example, in 1982, a Schools Council exploratory study into options operating in 10 schools asked 228 fourth-formers how they reached their decisions about option choices. They were presented with 11 factors that might have helped them choose. For each factor pupils were asked to consider six possible replies graded from the highly positive 'YES!' to the very negative 'NO!'. The table below presents the items receiving positive reactions in rank order.

Table 27:   Influences affecting choice of options

Rank order	Influences	Total no. of positive tallies
1	Parents	150
2	Teachers	136
3	School option information	132
4	Books, leaflets	103
5	Career talks	86
6	Other adults	74
7	Brothers or sisters	69
8	Career interviews	56
9	Friends	53
10	Newspaper or magazine articles	37
11	TV or radio programmes	31

SOURCE: Schools Council (Bardell, 1982).

Numerically at least, advice from parents, school option information

and teachers was significantly more influential than contacts with
friends or messages through the media. How important, therefore, for
the language departments to guarantee that their subjects are presented in a correct light and to develop greater links with the
parents. It is also a matter of urgency for the language associations to produce more publicity literature, to play a part in the
campaign to encourage pupils of both sexes to continue beyond the
option stage. No careers convention should take place without a
strong presence by language staff. I also believe it important that
languages come to be an integral part of pre-vocational courses at
school level. Events such as the regionally-based Festivals of
Languages, initiated so successfully in the South West of England in
1984, can also serve to bring languages more into the public eye.

CILT has made an important contribution by producing an information
pack on Languages and careers which gives the language teacher,
adviser or careers officer ready access to up-to-date information
which can be passed on to pupils and parents (Hewett, 1986).

Perhaps the publication of this Guide will also serve to alert the
profession to the need for action now. There is plenty of work to be
done!

Pupil-focussed remedies

* Making languages 'fun' without developing a coherent programme
  of learning will act only as a short-term palliative. Nonetheless, teachers should heed pupil warnings that lessons are 'boring' and strive to stimulate increased interest and enjoyment
  through greater variety, lively presentation and offering pupils
  a greater sense of involvement, achievement and progress.

* More encouragement should be given to pupils making non-
  traditional choices (i.e. boys taking languages) and special
  support for minority sex-groups should be sustained.

* Pupils' pre-conceptions of sex-roles should be challenged inside
  and outside the classroom.

* The syllabus for the third year should not be so influenced by
  the examinations in the fifth year as to become a dull grammar-
  based course.

* Teachers should not pressurise pupils into performing in front
  of their peers.

* Teachers should plan their lessons so that activities requiring
  intense concentration are interspersed with more relaxed activities.

* The language associations should produce posters, photographs,

displays of advertisements, job descriptions, accounts of work experience and lists of speakers, etc to enable departments to publicise the importance of their subjects at the time of option choice.

* Language departments should examine all the materials produced by the school in the lead-up to option choices to ensure that foreign and community languages are given proper treatment.

* Schools should encourage their pupils to take part in events such as the Young Linguists Competition and the Festival of Languages and involve the local press and radio in broadcasting the pupils' work and achievements.

Conclusion

When discussing policy matters in the context of gender issues in the comprehensive school, one writer felt inclined, albeit in a knowingly facetious way, to recommend the setting up of a pressure group specifically to encourage more boys to study languages (Davies, 1984). There have, after all, been several 'sister' projects such as GIST (Girls into Science and Technology) and GAMMA (Girls and Mathematics Association), so she hit upon the impressive sounding 'Boys and Learning Languages Society'. If ever such a body were to be created, I would hope that some less provocative acronym would result from the title! Maybe, seriously, it is time to campaign more vigorously, to draw attention to the increasing sex differentiation in languages. Were some monitoring group to emerge out of growing concern, possibly through the Joint Council of Language Associations or as a part of the work of the National Congress on Languages in Education, I would probably wish to apply for membership. But that has not been my purpose in producing this Guide.

Let us imagine that such an organisation were created and that it were, by concerted effort, somehow to persuade more boys to take up languages into and beyond the fourth year. That would not necessarily mean that the climate of opinion in schools and society would change overnight. The topic which has been our focus cannot and should not be seen in isolation. I have endeavoured to show, by referring to more general aspects of the equality of opportunity debate, that current practice in schools and the hidden curriculum of opinions, preconceptions, expectations and advice that sustains it work to the detriment of both sexes.

It is significant that Her Majesty's Inspectorate has considered it important to pursue its own investigations in this field and contribute to discussions by publishing its report Boys and modern languages (HMI, 1985a). This follows the earlier, admittedly more impressively produced Matters for Discussion document on Girls and science published in 1980 (HMI, 1980). Interest and good intentions expressed at national level represent a valid starting point, but responsibility lies with all teachers in their daily dealings with their pupils. It is vital now that approaches to eliminating the sex bias in languages should be seen as part of a school's general aims geared to equalising opportunity for boys and girls. Both boys and girls risk being further disadvantaged in their education if a foreign language is no longer deemed an appropriate element in the curriculum of both sexes.

Bibliography

This bibliography contains only those works cited in the text. CILT holds a more extensive bibliography (compiled 1985) of volumes and articles on the general theme of sex differences and languages. Copies are available on request.

BARDELL, G (1982). Options for the fourth. London: Schools Council.

BESWICK, C (1976). Mixed or single-sex for French? Audio-Visual Language Journal, vol 14, no. 1, p 34-38.

BRIMER, M A (1969). Sex differences in listening comprehension. Journal of Research and Development in Education, vol 3, p 72-79.

BRITISH OVERSEAS TRADE BOARD STUDY GROUP ON FOREIGN LANGUAGES (1979). Foreign languages for overseas trade. London: BOTB.

BUCKBY, M (1976). Is primary French really in the balance? Audio-Visual Language Journal, vol 14, no. 1, p 15-21.

BUCKBY, M (1979). Teaching pupils of lower ability: attitudes in the classroom. Audio-Visual Language Journal, vol 17, no. 2, p 77-82.

BUCKBY, M (1981). Graded objectives and tests for modern languages: an evaluation. London: Schools Council.

BURSTALL, C et al (1974). Primary French in the balance. Windsor: NFER.

CARROLL, J B (1975). The teaching of French as a foreign language in eight countries. Stockholm: Almqvist & Wiksell.

CHETWYND, J and O Hartnett, eds (1978). The sex-role system. London: Routledge & Kegan Paul.

CLWYD COUNTY COUNCIL (1983). Equal opportunities and the secondary school curriculum. Final report. Clwyd: Clwyd County Council/Equal Opportunities Commission.

COUNCIL OF EUROPE SECRETARIAT (1982). Sex-stereotyping in schools. Report on an Educational Research Workshop held at Hønefoss, May 1981. Lisse: Swets & Zeitlinger.

DALE, R R (1974). Mixed or single-sex school? Vol III. London: Routledge & Kegan Paul.

DAVIES, L and R Meigham (1975). A review of schooling and sex roles. *Educational Review*, vol 27, no. 3, p 165–78.

DAVIES, L (1984). Gender and comprehensive schooling . In S Ball, ed. *Comprehensive schooling: a reader*. Brighton: Falmer Press.

DEEM, R (1978). *Women and schooling*. London: Routledge & Kegan Paul.

DEEM, R, ed (1984). *Co-education reconsidered*. Milton Keynes: Open University Press.

DELAMONT, S (1980). *Sex roles and the school*. London: Methuen.

DEPARTMENT OF EDUCATION AND SCIENCE, (1983). *Foreign languages in the school curriculum*. (A consultative paper.) London: DES/Welsh Office.

EARDLEY, M (1984). Language study in the sixth form: an attitude survey. *British Journal of Language Teaching*, vol 22, no. 1, p 3–8.

EQUAL OPPORTUNITIES COMMISSION (1983). *Equal opportunities: what's in it for boys?* Manchester: EOC.

GAFF, R (1982). Sex-stereotyping in modern language teaching – an aspect of the hidden curriculum. *British Journal of Language Teaching*, vol 22, no. 2, p 71–78.

GUTTENTAG, M and H Bray (1976). *Undoing sex stereotypes*. New York: McGraw-Hill.

HANDLEY, P (1984). *Adult education and the teaching of languages: the current situation in England and Wales*. Brighton: Language Centre, Brighton Polytechnic.

HARDING, J (1983). *Switched off: the science education of girls*. London: Longman for the Schools Council.

HARTMAN, P and E Judd (1978). Sexism and TESOL materials. *TESOL Quarterly*, vol 12, no. 4, p 383–93.

HAWKINS, E (1981). *Modern languages in the curriculum*. Cambridge: Cambridge University Press.

HER MAJESTY'S INSPECTORATE (HMI) (1975). *Curricular differences for boys and girls*. Education Survey no. 21. London: HMSO.

HMI (1980). *Girls and science*. London: HMSO.

HMI (1985a). *Boys and modern languages*. Inspection report. London: Department of Education and Science.

HMI (1985b). Modern languages in the sixth form. Inspection report. London: Department of Education and Science.

Hewett, D, ed (1986). Languages and careers: an information pack. London: Centre for Information on Language Teaching and Research.

HIRST, G (1982). An evaluation of evidence for innate sex differences in linguistic ability. Journal of Psycholinguistic Research, vol 11, no. 2, p 95-113.

HUTT, C (1972). Males and females. Harmondsworth: Penguin.

ILEA ANTI-SEXIST WORKING PARTY (1984). Equal opportunities - gender: guidelines for teachers of languages. London: ILEA Modern Language Centre.

KLANN-DELIUS, G (1981). Sex and language acquisition. Is there any influence? Journal of Pragmatics, vol 5, p 1-25.

KNAPMAN, D (1982). School-associated anxieties. Somerset: Somerset Education Department.

MACAULAY, R K S (1978). The myth of female superiority in language. Journal of Child Language, vol 5, no. 2, p 353-363.

MACCOBY, E E, ed (1967). The development of sex differences. London: Tavistock.

MACCOBY, E E and C N Jacklin (1974). The psychology of sex differences. Stanford: Stanford University Press.

MARLAND, M, ed (1983). Sex differentiation and schooling. London: Heinemann.

MORRIS, P D (1978). Children's attitudes to French at 13+. Modern Languages, vol 59, no. 4, p 177-183.

MOYS, A et al (1980). Modern languages examinations at sixteen plus: a critical analysis. London: CILT.

NEWSOM REPORT (1963). Central Advisory Council for Education. Half our future. (The Newsom Report.) London: HMSO.

NORWOOD REPORT (1943). Board of Education Secondary Schools Examinations Council on Curriculum and examinations in secondary schools. (The Norwood Report) London: HMSO.

O'BRIEN, J (1985). The modern language image. Upublished MEd Dissertation. Nottingham: University of Nottingham.

PARTINGTON, J and P Luker (1984). Teaching modern languages: a teaching skills workbook. London: Macmillan.

POWELL, R C and P Littlewood (1982). Foreign languages. The avoidable options. British Journal of Language Teaching, vol 20, no. 3, p 153-59.

POWELL, R C and J D Batters (1985). Pupils' perceptions of foreign language learning at 12+: some gender differences. Educational Studies, vol 11, no. 1, p 11-23.

PRATT, J, J Bloomfield and C Seale (1984). Option choice. A question of equal opportunity. Windsor: NFER-Nelson.

RIDING, R J and D L T Vincent (1980). Listening comprehension: the effects of sex, age, passage structure and speech rate. Educational Review, vol 32, no. 3, p 259-266.

SMITH, S (1984). Single-sex setting. In R Deem, ed. Co-education reconsidered. Milton Keynes: Open University Press.

SPENDER, D (1982). Invisible women: the schooling scandal. London: Writers and Readers.

STANWORTH, M (1983). Gender and schooling: a study of sexual divisions in the classroom. London: Hutchinson in association with the Explorations in Feminism Collective.

STOCKARD, J et al (1980). Sex equity in education. New York: Academic Press.

SUTHERLAND, M (1981). Sex bias in education. Oxford: Blackwell.

WESTGATE, D et al. (1985). Some characteristics of interaction in foreign language classrooms. British Educational Research Journal, vol 11, no. 3, p 271-281.

WHYLD, J, ed (1983). Sexism in the secondary curriculum. London: Harper & Row.

WHYTE, J (1984). Observing sex stereotypes and interactions in the school lab and workshop. Educational Review, vol 36, no. 1, p 75-86.

WHYTE, J (1985). Girls into science and technology. London: Routledge & Kegan Paul.

WITTIG, M A and A C Peterson, eds (1979). Sex related differences in cognitive functioning. New York: Academic Press.